Contents

ISBN 0-87666-561-X

© Copyright 1983 by T.F.H. Publications, Inc., Ltd.

Distributed in the UNITED STATES by T.F.H. Publications, Inc., 211 West Sylvania Avenue, Neptune City, NJ 07753; in CANADA by H & L Pet Supplies Inc., 27 Kingston Crescent, Kitchener, Ontario N2B 2T6; Rolf C. Hagen Ltd., 3225 Sartelon Street, Montreal 382 Quebec; in ENGLAND by T.F.H. (Great Britain) Ltd., 11 Ormside Way, Holmethorpe Industrial Estate, Redhill, Surrey RH1 2PX; in AUSTRALIA AND THE SOUTH PACIFIC by T.F.H. (Australia) Pty. Ltd., Box 149, Brookvale 2100 N.S.W., Australia; in NEW ZEALAND by Ross Haines & Son, Ltd., 18 Monmouth Street, Grey Lynn, Auckland 2 New Zealand; in SINGAPORE AND MALAYSIA by MPH Distributors Pte., 71-77 Stamford Road, Singapore 0617; in the PHILIPPINES by Bio-Research, 5 Lippay Street, San Lorenzo Village, Makati, Rizal; in SOUTH AFRICA by Multipet Pty. Ltd., 30 Turners Avenue, Durban 4001. Published by T.F.H. Publications Inc., Ltd., the British Crown Colony of Hong Kong.

The T.F.H. Book of
SNAKES

t.f.h.

Thomas Leetz

Preface

Having been raised in rural southwestern Michigan, finding snakes during the spring and summer months was a natural occurrence. Luckily, I was fortunate to have parents who encouraged my interests and never indoctrinated me with fears and misconceptions about snakes.

Combined with curing the snake-hater, being able to share my knowledge with aspiring "serpentologists" has been my goal fulfilled. If one person finds this book of use, then all my efforts have had a purpose.

This book is not intended for the professional or the already successful hobbyist. Rather, it is my contention that it should be used by the novice of any age who wishes to begin a satisfying endeavor that will credit itself with learning and enjoyment.

I wish to dedicate this book to my parents, Norman and Lenore, and also to my sister Janice, all of whom provided motivation, patience, and patronage when I needed it the most; to my many friends and herptile mates such as Professor David Synder, Mr. and Mrs. Raymond Byrd, the entire Ellis family, the Great Lakes Herpetological Society, and others too numerous to mention, friends who have realized all along that ideas and wisdom shared are the formula for success; to my wonderful wife, Donna, without whose love and devotion there would be no book or reason to write it; and, lest I forget, to the many professional herpetologists who have served as role models in my life since I was a young boy. Special thanks are due to Mr. Jeff Gee and Mr. Michael Fitzgerald for their devoted help and knowledgeable contributions and to Mr. and Mrs. William E. Bufalino for their special encouragement.

Corn snakes are often recommended as "first snakes" for beginning hobbyists because of their attractive patterns and colors, docile temperament, and ready availability at low prices. However, they require warm-blooded food such as mice or chicks, and many individuals never become accustomed to accepting frozen and thawed mice, demanding living food. Photo by Ken Lucas at Steinhart Aquarium.

Serpent Politics

Fear is a highly personal and individualized form of ignorance. Or, to put it another way, people who refuse to deal rationally with an unknown seem to develop their fears simply due to the fact of not being aware of or taking the time to learn about the feared object, when actual knowledge and not hearsay would cure any fear, real or contrived. Now this is not intended to claim that all who fear certain things or act cautiously are uneducated. We all have fears, and sometimes for good reasons. Unfortunately, we let strong emotions and discrimination block our judgment; we will always tend to act as humans. You may ask, why the lesson in psychology in a snake book? To explain this I must remember my childhood. Throughout my school days I was a physical "late bloomer" of very small and fragile build. Never having the strength and effectiveness of my male peers, I was frequently an outcast in sporting and physical events. What amazed me was the reactions I would receive from some of my friends when I would approach them with a reptile, especially a snake, no matter how diminutive. These animals, which seemed such a normal fact of life to me, could strike fear in the minds of others, some many times my age and size.

I do not wish to advocate that people deliberately scare others with snakes as a sign of power. This is not my point, though there does seem to be a lesson to be learned. In our own right, though, snake hobbyists do command a certain amount of respect. Looking at my example, it's easy to see that the only true power lies in being educated about snakes and taking advantage of those who are not. Sometimes, I might add, this was not a reaction of fear but of disinterest. Having purchased this book, you obviously have an interest in snakes and may have recognized this type of behavior in others. Assuredly we snake handlers are in a class by ourselves. Try to make it your goal to educate others who display curiosity and relieve those who suffer from "ophidiophobia" (fear of snakes).

For most people the average day is filled with the hustle and bustle of routine living. Rarely are the aspects of our natural world given a moment's thought. A few may by chance happen to glimpse a snake, usually dead, while driving down isolated suburban roads. Other than this, the majority of the public will view snakes only while visiting the zoo. A chance encounter between most people and a snake will bring forth unwarranted fear and an overwhelming sense that the animal should, for some vague reason, be destroyed.

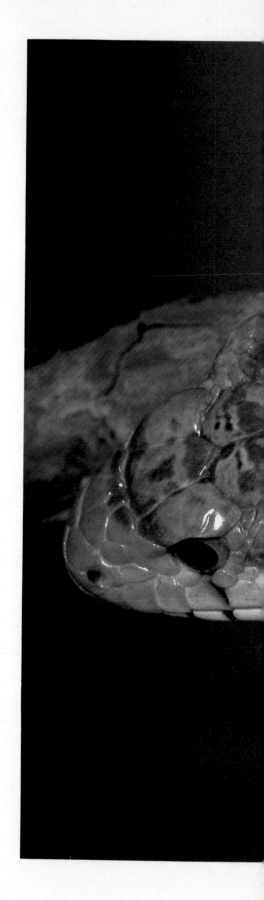

Two-headed animals are usually caused by accidents affecting the developing embryo at an early stage of life. For some reason, there seem to be more two-headed snakes and turtles around than any other types of animals. This stunning photo of a two-headed gopher snake shows why such specimens are greatly valued as display animals by zoos and museums. Photo by Ken Lucas at Steinhart Aquarium.

To ask someone to define the word cat or dog would gather surprise and wonderment at being asked a seemingly unneccessary and obvious question. Yet to question most people about snakes, even in these modern days of technological advancement, would elicit some wild and exaggerated responses. What then are the positive benefits to having snakes in our daily lives? Little, actually. It's the long-range effects that must be examined. A farmer can tell you the advantages of finding snakes in his barns and fields as opposed to finding an abundance of mice and other pests that can over-run needed crops. Snakes have also entered the laboratory and are now being used in chemotherapy and radiation research. Isn't it comforting to know that all the earthly creatures exist not only for themselves, but as part of a complex scheme where balance is dependent upon the survival of others? Furthermore, just because the snake's nature does not seem to relate directly to the "human factor," should this indicate the need for eradication? Who knows what hidden benefits may be derived from later, yet unknown, uses of snakes.

Even worse than snake haters, in my opinion, are the people who kill and sell snakes for quick monetary gain. Today we still have rattlesnake round-ups where snakes are killed by the thousands to make boots, belts, hat bands, and other assorted useless trinkets. There are zoological black market salesmen who sell endangered species of all types. These profiteers care little about the damaging effects they cause and are only interested in money.

Now let's turn our attention to the development of the whole focal point of this book, the snake. All school children realize that snakes are reptiles. What is incompletely known is when and how the modern snake came into being. It is generally accepted that the snakes evolved from lizards, but little has been left in the way of fossilized remains to document their actual development. Only theories proposed by paleontologists and herpetologists will have to suffice until new and more detailed findings give us a definitive answer.

Of all the reptiles, snakes are my favorites. Not being one to accept mythology or possessing deep religious convictions, I tend to look toward science for my explanations, though I must admit there is a bit of magic in keeping and studying snakes. They have long served as symbols of both good and evil, being both worshiped and reviled. Snakes have always seemed to figure in the legends of man's past, whether to explain a common meteorological event in mythology, the use of the demonic serpent in the Garden of Eden in our own Judeo-Christian ethic, or on the "Don't Tread on Me" banner used in America during the struggle

Thamnophis sirtalis sirtalis, the common eastern garter snake, is usually one of the first snakes seen by children in the eastern U.S., and very similar species and subspecies are abundant from coast to coast. This 2- to 3-foot species manages to thrive even in vacant lots of large cities. Photo by Ken Lucas at Steinhart Aquarium.

In the southern U.S., the gray rat snake, *Elaphe obsoleta spiloides,* is often called a "chicken snake" because it frequents the vicinity of chicken houses and often eats eggs (thus the common name "egg snake"). Although often killed on sight as vermin, it is actually an important predator on mice, sparrows, and other pests. Photo by Ken Lucas at Steinhart Aquarium.

against the British during the American Revolution. Snakes even today seem to retain portions of this magic.

As you can see, being a herpetological hobbyist is more than just another pastime. It's obvious that you are ready to embark upon your own selection for study. After all, that's the intended purpose of this book. You provide the enthusiasm, and I will provide selection suggestions and keeping and maintenance tips. This way you will gain knowledge, and that will fuel the desire for advanced study.

As you read on you will note that I have offered a mixture of natural history, useful facts, hints on husbandry, and personal philosophy. Trying to achieve a well-balanced portion of each part was another intention of mine when I wrote this book. With this in mind, please realize that when dealing with animal care and abiding by set principles from others, you will find much of it to be relative. The following procedures have worked well for me and for many of my herptile associates. I hope you enjoy the same success, but don't be afraid to experiment and use your own judgment.

I wish I could pinpoint what your exact monetary outlay will be in getting started, but there are too many variables. First of all, you may or may not already have an adequate cage. Secondly, you may wish to breed your own food items. Also, do you intend to catch a snake or purchase one? As you can now understand, there is no one correct answer, but as you may expect it will generally be less expensive than keeping your average dog or cat. Be mindful not to underestimate the value of supplying your pet with the best quality care. Remember that your pet is doing you a service—you wanted to keep it, it didn't want to be kept.

I heartily recommend further reading. I can not supply you with total serpent knowledge in one book. Take advantage of the many other titles on the market and available in any bookstore. As your skill develops, so will your need for broader and more advanced reading.

First of all, how do you intend to acquire your snake? If you opt to purchase one from a petshop or zoological supplier you will definitely have the benefit of varied and exotic selections. Also, you will be at an advantage by having direct contact with knowledgeable personnel and possibly a limited warranty. Unfortunately you also will have to pay a price. This may well be worth it when you consider the fact that you will have little sacrifice except to hand-select your pet. You are purchasing an animal that will, with proper care, live a long life.

Still, you may be a naturalist who enjoys the skill involved in snake collecting; most herpetologists are. First it is necessary to know the serpent fauna that can be found in your area and what type of snake you want. It will do you

no good to be prepared to house one type and end up bringing home another or to go out looking day after day only to realize eventually that the snake you want is indigenous to environments far away. Be patient—it is not uncommon to spend all day looking and go home empty-handed. Following the simple rules below will cut down the margin for error.

In the continental U.S., snakes can be found in every state but are most diverse and abundant in the warmer southern and southwestern regions. In the North, snakes will hibernate during the winter; look for them in the early spring, especially during mating season, when they will be very active and not as secretive. It is logical that you should search for water snakes near water, where they are inclined to spend 95% of their time, and for terrestrial snakes under logs, stacked wood, and rocks. The best hours to collect snakes are during the day, preferably early morning when it's still cool and the snakes emerge to bask in the sun on rocks, grass, or pavement. Catching your pet during the early morning when it's cool also has the advantage that normally nervous specimens that may be prone to biting are more docile and react more slowly. Having lower body temperatures and thus slower reaction times and a more docile temperament also will help in acclimating your new pet to human contact. Should you collect in habitats where poisonous snakes are found, or if catching one is your objective, always venture out with someone else and never alone. The outcome of a mistake or an accident to a solitary collector is often more serious than if a companion were available to help.

Before you begin your hunt, secure permission from all landowners on whose property you wish to search. If you remain on your own boundries or those of friends there can be no disputes, but every year well-intentioned hobbyists

Snakes are seldom easy to spot in their natural habitats. The various stripes, blotches, diamonds, and fleckings of color serve to make them blend into the background. Rocky desert snakes such as the night snake, *Hypsiglena torquata* (above), are seldom collected except when warming themselves on roads at night. Copperheads, *Agkistrodon contortrix,* have color patterns that resemble the dried pine needles in which they are commonly found (below). Photo above by Ken Lucas at Steinhart Aquarium; photo below by Jeff Gee.

Old barns (above) are often good places to find snakes such as rat snakes, corn snakes, and racers, but they are often dangerous or on private property. The open stands of pine that characterize many parts of the southern U.S. have many snake species (below), but the hunting is often hot, thirsty work, with individual snakes uncommon and insects abundant. Photos by Jeff Gee.

overlook this basic rule and end up doing a lot of explaining and help give snake hunters a poor reputation. Until you are positive about the collecting laws and reptiles deemed endangered in a specific locale, make no attempts at collecting. Such laws vary from state to state and usually are strictly enforced. When in doubt, contact your local fish and game authority. Have respect for these laws and understand that they were introduced for good reason to protect the fauna. These laws are constantly being updated and either strengthened or relaxed as the situation warrants. One final point that can usually go without being mentioned—honor the sacred ground on which you tread. Do not be disruptive, litter, or be careless. Remember that you are a guest in the animals' home. Leave the area just as you found it.

Once you have acquired your snake, whether it is caught or purchased, be wise and always use correct handling procedures. Be gentle; don't manhandle your pet. Always cradle its weight and support its entire body. Avoid extreme amounts of handling, and never let someone who is inexperienced handle the snake or force someone who is frightened to hold the animal. When you are with your pet, give it your total attention. Be careful not to pinch or overexcite the snake. Even when approaching harmless species that will bite, I recommend using gloves and other protective clothing rather than employing the old standard pinch hold that puts pressure just behind the jaws at the back of the skull. Although the situation sometimes will necessitate the use of this method, for beginers it is just an accident waiting to happen as far as the snake is concerned.

Noticeable during your snake's captive tenure will be a large capacity to display emotional character and mood. Just as we and all other animals tend to exhibit fear, boredom, anxiety, curiosity, and so on, so will your snake. After a period of time you will become conscious of some of these moods, and many will act as indicators to govern your behavior as a concerned keeper. For example, many of my snakes will become overly anxious and irritable if regular feeding time is overlooked. When my snakes do not want to be bothered they act sullen and shy, and in some cases they prefer to hide for as much as three or four days consecutively. Your snake will come to recognize you as its captor and feeder. Though snakes are usually considered to be of low intelligence, the fact should not be overlooked that snakes are capable of training in the form of feeding, housing, and overcoming fear. These traits are accomplished through the use of conditioned responses. Usage of such basic traits is the first requisite for measuring intelligence in higher animals.

What is a Snake?

CHARACTERISTICS

Snakes all belong to the order Squamata ("the scaly ones"). This order is comprised of both lizards and snakes, with the superficial differences between the two being obvious. Snakes, suborder Serpentes, of which there are approximately 2,000 species worldwide, are very successful reptiles and have a wider distribution than any other living group of reptiles. Found in xeric (desert) to fully aquatic habitats, they reside as far north as Canada, the Arctic Circle in Eurasia, and in high mountains, but only five of the 12 families often recognized occur in the U.S., consisting of some 250 species and subspecies.

Characteristically, snakes lack functional limbs. The boids possess vestigial hind legs in the form of movable spurs located on each side of the vent. Never used in locomotion, the spurs are connected to pelvic bone remnants (which are not attached to the spinal column) by cartilage. They are remnants of the evolutionary past, retained from lizard ancestors.

Having no outer ear or tympanic membrane, snakes gather vibrations through the substrate. The inner ear bones articulate with the quadrate bone that is attached by ligaments to the lower jaw and skull. Little is known about just how the vibrations are actually perceived by the snake.

A snake's olfactory sense is more acute than its sight. A snake's vision is marginal. Because the eyes are on the sides of the head, only one eye can focus on a subject at a time (some vine snakes may have binocular vision). A hard spectacle (the brille) covering the eye and nonmovable eyelids give the snakes their hypnotic glare. Even though most snakes lack depth perception, tests have determined that their eyes contain cones in the retinas, so snakes probably can perceive color.

Most snakes are crepuscular, hunting for food during the pre-dawn hours. Nocturnal species often have elliptical pupils and comparatively good sight in darkness. Snakes usually lack effective sight beyond about 10 feet.

The teeth of snakes are usually small and curved backward. Most have dual rows in the upper jaws and single rows in the bottom jaws that are extremely sharp and serve in holding prey. Both halves of a snake's mandibles (lower jaws) are attached by ligaments to the skull at the back and to each other by another ligament at the front. This makes them extremely flexible to allow passage of food that may be comparatively large in size.

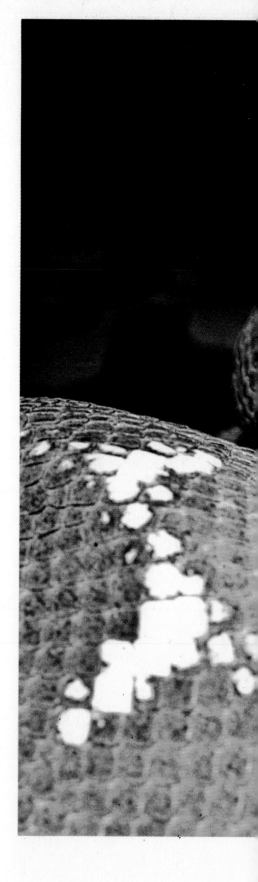

The elliptical pupil of the eye identifies this green tree boa, *Corallus caninus,* as a nocturnal hunter. The deep pits in the scales along the upper jaw (the upper labials) help the snake sense warm-blooded prey such as tree-dwelling rodents and bird nests even in the dark. The bright green color and tendency to coil into a ball on a convenient branch during the day help prevent it from being spotted by enemies during the day.

Combined with, but separate from, the regular olfactory sense is the Jacobson's organ. Rapid "flicking" motions of the forked tongue enable the snake to pick up odorous particles from the air and ground. These particles are returned to the mouth, where they are passed along sensitive nerve endings in the base of the maxilla (the Jacobson's organ) and sorted to give the snake the desired information. This organ is not used just for food location, but also helps in forming hibernation groups and in locating partners during mating season.

Pit vipers and several pythons and boas are equipped with an additional system for detecting prey. Just below and behind the nostrils of pit vipers and along the lip line of some boas and pythons there exist pits lined with sensory cells that are designed to detect radiant heat even in total darkness. Adaptions such as this have made snakes excellent hunters and trackers.

Depending on the species, snakes employ differing modes of locomotion. Heavy-bodied snakes, such as the constrictors and large rattlers, will use rectilineation or caterpillar movement, using their broad ventral scales to propel themselves forward much like tire treads. This allows even distribution of weight alternately along several points. Other snakes, especially the slim-bodied colubrids, will use serpentine or "S"-shaped movements. In this case pressure is put against exposed objects, grass, sticks, or the substrate by the edges of the body to produce this very familiar style of movement. This motion, incidentaly, is used by all snakes when swimming. Concertina motion is produced by compacting the body into coils and, with the tail anchored, surging forward to start the process over again. Also familiar is side-winding, as demonstrated by the southwestern American sidewinder rattlesnake and the North African horned viper. This method is highly effective for moving across desert sand. With its head extended, the snake moves obliquely, touching the ground in only two places and managing to throw forward each successive loop of its body.

Snakes, like all other living reptiles, are considered to be "cold-blooded" or, more correctly, poikilothermic. Their body temperature varies with that of their surroundings, but they can control their body temperature to some extent by basking and other behavior. Too much heat or direct sunlight without being able to escape as well as excessively low temperatures both have adverse or even deadly effects. Minor amounts of heat are produced through muscular contractions in nesting pythons, but this is very rare in snakes.

Throughout its lifetime a snake continues to grow, though after sexual maturity is reached the process of shedding will decrease considerably. At regular intervals controlled by eating habits, hormones, and metabolism, a snake will slough its entire outer layer of skin. Approximately ten days prior to the actual shedding (which may only require one hour) the first signs may be seen. Swelling of the head caused by an increase in blood pressure initiates the separating of the old layer of skin from the new layer below by a layer of lymph. Generally, snakes shed their entire skin at one time, turning it inside out. When the shedding process nears, you will notice that your snake's colors will become dusty and muted. The spectacles covering the eyes will become cloudy or even turn blue. When this takes place your snake may become edgy and resist handling. This reaction is due to the fact that their eyesight is greatly diminished, which out in the wild would make the snake particularly vulnerable. Your snake may be apt to frequent its water dish for extra soaking periods, so it will be important for you to keep the dish clean and full. After a few days you will notice that the spectacles become clear again. Following this, in about two days the actual shedding will begin due to involuntary physiological changes, and the skin will separate and be easily removed by the snake, usually by rubbing against rocks or limbs. Upon completion of the shed, the dermis may be removed from the cage and discarded, or it can be saved for study.

Snakes have separate sexes, and a few are sexually dimorphic in scale counts or details of the color pattern. The male has a paired sex organ called the hemipenes that is located in pouches at the base of the tail just behind the vent and emerges from the cloaca. Females are inseminated through direct copulation, the male inserting only one hemipenis during mating. Snakes develop in two similar but superficially different ways. About half the colubrids and most elapids (cobras, etc.) are oviparous, laying eggs. On the other hand, the vipers, pit vipers, and about half the colubrids are ovoviviparous, bearing living young. In ovoviviparous snakes the egg (without a shell) is retained in the body of the female and the young develop internally, feeding on the egg yolk. In truly viviparous snakes (a few water snakes are thought to be truly viviparous) there is a placenta connecting the developing young to the mother's blood supply, and the embryo is actually given nutriment from the mother's body. After an initial mating, females can store sperm and become pregnant for several more seasons even without further copulation. This process of sperm retention and delayed fertilization is not uncommon and has evolved to ensure successful propagation in species

This baby water snake, *Nerodia sipedon,* was only recently born. Like other American water snakes, the eggs of this species are retained in the body of the mother until hatching occurs and are only covered with thin membranes, not shells. As the hatching actually happens in the body of the mother or immediately after the egg is passed from the body, the snake appears to give live birth although the mother does nothing to provide nourishment for the developing egg. *Nerodia* species are thus said to be ovoviviparous (egg-live-bearing would be a literal if horrible translation). The very similar Eurasian water snakes, genus *Natrix,* actually lay shelled eggs and are oviparous (eggbearing). Photo courtesy American Museum of Natural History.

18

The intricately patterned Dumeril's boa, *Acrantophis dumerilii*, is found only in a small region of Madagascar and is likely to become extinct in the near future if not protected from human intrusion. Although boas in general are primitive snakes, they are still usually very specialized to fill a particular niche in an undisturbed habitat. Man-made changes in habitat or predation on the often small populations as specimens for the pet trade may sometimes cause the species to cease reproducing and eventually die out. Photo by Ken Lucas at Steinhart Aquarium.

with small populations where mates are not always easy to find.

Anatomically, snakes are not totally symmetrical. The paired organs, such as the kidneys, lung or lungs, and gonads, commonly have one side reduced or even absent (most snakes have only one lung, for instance) to ease accommodation in the elongated body. The snakes have three-chambered hearts that are less efficient than four-chambered hearts because oxygenated and deoxygenated blood are mixed. Few snakes have a great deal of stamina in the sense that they cannot glide readily for long distances at full speed.

SPECIALIZATIONS

To the casual observer it would seem that snakes are severely handicapped. After all, they have no legs and arms, and their existence is apparently limited to a belly's-height

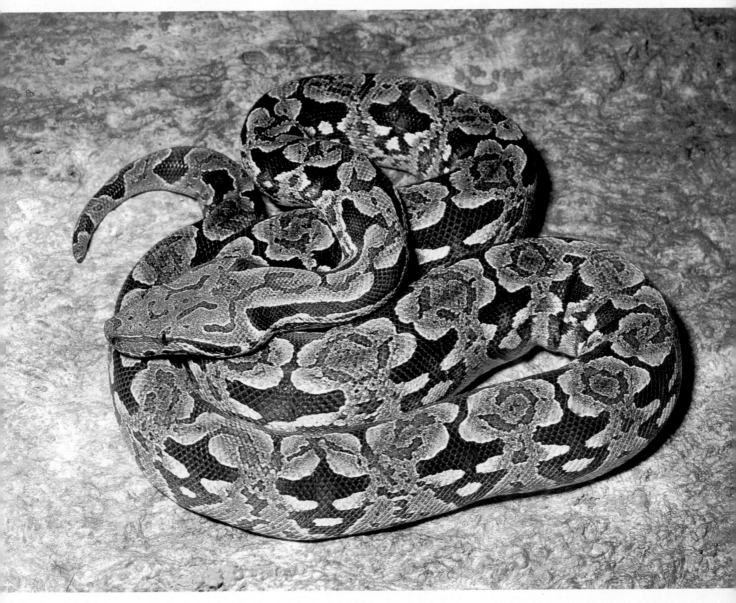

from the ground. Actually, such reasoning could not be farther from the truth. Snakes are the authorities on specialization. Indeed, it is probably the lack of legs that has allowed snakes to exploit habitats that other animals could not inhabit.

Snakes are all limbless, all are of elongate form, and all are cold-blooded. However, this is where macro similarities end and the micro begin. The types of habitats utilized, unusual body structures, and adaptations for finding and feeding on certain prey animals have all helped determine exactly how snakes look and how the species differ from each other.

No doubt everyone is familiar with the boas and pythons and the fact that they constrict their prey. To most people the mention of constricting conjures up the thought that one of these evil creatures lies in wait for some hapless animal to stumble upon the snake's lair, where it is squeezed into pulpy mush and then zealously eaten. In reality only part of this story is true. Yes, the snake does employ quickness and stealth in achieving its kill, but more prey probably will escape than will be caught. As the name "constrictor" would imply, great strength is exerted, but bones are seldom broken. Only when the excited prey exhales do the muscles constrict tighter, and in reality the intended victim suffocates. This process is quick and probably relatively painless. Many colubrids (typical snakes) such as the rat snakes and kingsnakes also make use of this method.

Some pythons and boas have adapted to climbing and normally live in the trees, rarely descending and subsisting totally upon birds and other tree-dwelling animals. Not only do many boids take to the trees, but so do many species of graceful and slender vine snakes. So thin are the vine snakes that they can glide along even the thinnest branch without weighing it down. Even some poisonous snakes are arboreal, like the green eyelash viper that has a prehensile tail that can wind around tree branches and has reflexes so fast it can catch birds in flight.

Amazing as these adaptations seem, there are still more. Nature has seen fit to bestow upon snakes the fine arts of both display colors and camouflage. The spectacled cobra can spread its hood and intimidate most of its enemies. The harmless milk snakes have brilliant red, yellow, and black rings on the body that resemble coral snake color patterns. Countless other snakes have skin patterns that blend easily with their backgrounds. Vine snakes are once more an example—they may attain a length of 4 feet, yet they blend remarkably well with the foliage and can remain motionless for hours.

The very strong but flexible body of the green tree boa allows it to live continuously in the trees and seldom come to the ground. Many arboreal (tree-dwelling) snakes are similar in color and shape: bright green, with long, slender bodies, long tails, and an often triangular cross-section to the body. Photo by Dr. Marcos A. Freiberg.

Extremes in snakes. The sea snake (above) is adapted to live only in the sea and feeds almost exclusively on eels, while the worm snake, *Leptotyphlops humilis* (below), burrows only in or near ant and termite nests and feeds only on the most delicate prey. Photo below by Ken Lucas at Steinhart Aquarium.

Of course, it would not be proper to ignore the most notorious of all snake adaptations, venom. Venomous snakes occur in most countries, from the U.S. and Europe to Australia and Fiji. They may be as small as 12 inches, as in the case of the pygmy rattlers, or as large as 18 feet, as in the king cobra. Some contain poisons with the ability to destroy the tissues or clot the blood, while others destroy or damage the nervous system.

In several instances it appears as if the entire form of the animal were built to conform to its environment. One such group of snakes is the elusive sea snakes. Rather complacent serpents, they are poisonous, and their bites are frequently fatal. These snakes usually bear living young, and in doing so they never have to leave the water. Their small heads and rudder-like tails, combined with the ability to remain submerged for extended periods of time, make them prime examples of the snakes' ability to be at home under almost any conditions.

Thus far we have examined snakes that are experts on land, in the trees, and in the water. It is only fitting that there are also snakes that are burrowers (fossorial) and suited for subterranean living. The blind snake families (Leptotyphlopidae, Anomalepididae, and Typhlopidae), the iridescent shieldtails of India and Sri Lanka (Uropeltidae), and the South American pipe snakes (Aniliidae) are small burrowers (often less than 12 inches) and are highly secretive. Most species live in the tropics and feed mostly on ants and termites. The blind snakes are usually translucent brown to violet or black, while the pipesnakes are patterned in red and black rings like the coral snakes. The degenerate eyes of these snakes serve little or no function. The Typhlopidae are considered by some to be actually the remnants of a group of lizards that became so snake-like that it is almost impossible to tell them from the true snakes in details of the skeleton and soft anatomy.

We can be thankful that we live in a day and age when we are able to explore these exciting animals that have, without a doubt, attained their very zenith of development. Few other animals have enjoyed such extraordinary modifications to enable them to successfully adapt in their specific ecosystems.

Why Keep Snakes?

Aside from their esthetic beauty, snakes offer a wide variety of reasons for being kept as pets. Always among the star attractions at any zoo, snakes possess the ability to captivate curious on-lookers, young and old alike. While your pet will not exhibit affection as a dog or other common house pet might, many species adjust well to captivity and tolerate a moderate amount of handling.

Outfitting a cage, feeding, and cleaning can, with patience, be done with ease. Along with these routine duties can be coupled many hours of entertainment and enjoyable study. Maintaining an accurate log and diary of your pet's food intake, resting habits, and other behavior can be beneficial as well as interesting. Proper notes from the start will help point out any changes that should be made. Many keepers have found that with adequate care their pets have lived 10, 15, or even 20 years, occasionally even longer. Much is still to be learned about snakes. True understanding can not be totally gained from your reading unless you have the opportunity to experience snakes at first hand. This will be accomplished through housing one yourself.

Snakes, like other reptiles, offer a perfect substitute pet for those individuals who are afflicted with allergies to animals with fur or feathers. As far as I am aware, reptiles are completely non-allergenic.

If kept properly under the prescribed methods, snakes are hygienic. Little effort must be spent to keep snakes clean, as opposed to other animals that require bathing and brushing and that may defecate several times a day. The need to remove feces regularly to prevent possible spread of infection and to keep the cage odor-free is the main concern.

Snakes are quiet and unassuming. Aside from an occasional hiss from some or quiet scuttling sounds on the branches or rocks, not a sound will be heard. Although regular exercise is recommended and often necessary, cages do not have to be very large, so not much space will be used up. The cage will of course have to be larger if you have an adult boa, python, or other snake of unusually large size.

These are just a few of the practical reasons in favor of keeping snakes as pets. Throughout history snakes have had a certain mystique. They are still considered by many to be sacred and to have divine powers. They have undoubtedly been able to evoke emotion, pro or con, in all of us.

The very nature of this book is to recommend "easy to keep snakes" and to suggest suitable husbandry methods to ensure their survival. In the chapter on popular choices, where I will individually critique several commonly kept

Few animals can equal the glossy vitality exhibited by a healthy kingsnake. This particular specimen is a San Diego mountain kingsnake, *Lampropeltis zonata pulchra,* from California, a snake now protected by law but still highly prized by collectors. Like most kingsnakes, it prefers lizards, mice, chicks, and other living foods. Kingsnakes are usually a joy to handle, as the smooth, cool body feels like fine porcelain and most specimens have an excellent disposition that allows them to be handled with little fear of bites. Photo by Ken Lucas at Steinhart Aquarium.

Three common types of snakes. **Facing page, top:** A garter snake, *Thamnophis sirtalis infernalis,* from California, is fairly typical (though more colorful than most other subspecies) of its kind. **Facing page, bottom:** The bright red to orange belly of the ringneck snake, *Diadophis punctatus,* characterizes the species throughout the U.S., though the color of the back and the size of the ring behind the head vary considerably. **Above:** This all-brown water snake, *Nerodia* species, is probably a banded water snake, *Nerodia fasciata,* though dark adults of several common water snakes look very much alike and are often difficult to identify. Photos on facing page by Ken Lucas at Steinhart Aquarium; photo above by Jeff Gee.

types of snakes, the choices will be limited to mainly the families Colubridae and Boidae. This is not to say that individuals from the other families have not or can not be kept, but many are either rare, commercially unobtainable, of the highest degree in difficulty to house, or poisonous. I will not recommend any poisonous specimens because of their potential deadliness. Others can either not be handled, are to hard to find, or are simply uninteresting to the hobbyist. It is the hands-on experience with the typical snakes that makes snake keeping the hobby it truly is. By all means bear in mind that being considered "typical" or "common" is not intended to degrade the quality of the snake. Rather, it is meant to indicate the degree of difficulty with which hobbyists are usually able to keep them. This also is not to imply that the snakes listed in this book will be successfully kept by everyone in every instance. The phrase "easy to keep" is relative. Your success will be related to your ability to provide adequate care and the snake's own general attitude.

Snakes in Captivity

For the past decade the "snake for sale" trade has been on the rise. More and more people have come to know the enjoyment and excitement of owning one of these fascinating creatures. As with any wild animal, certain criteria for care and feeding must be met. In nature it would normally find food and water on its own, but the snake must now have this provided for it. Special attention must be paid to the correct climate and variations that will occur during the day and evening. Also, careful consideration must be given to your snake's individual environment. The microhabitat where your snake will spend most of its day will depend largely on your knowledge. Just as you would not create a desert sand terrarium for a tropical or marshland snake, you also would not deprive an arboreal tree-dweller of proper climbing lattices. Being a conscientious owner and paying attention in the beginning to these details will help prevent problems such as lethargy or lack of appetite. Other important considerations to take into account are whether other family members, roommates, tenants, or landlords have any objections; what type of food will have to be obtained for it; and how much room will be needed. Moreover, forethought must be given to these items BEFORE your pet is acquired.

SELECTING A SNAKE

A blend of careful thought and personal preference should be combined when choosing your snake. Many times an impatient hobbyist will acquire a snake because of its beautiful color or current availability, with little or no thought to the snake's temperament or habits. Soon the hobbyist finds he is faced with a pet that he not only dislikes but does not understand, and as with so many pets, the snake suffers until its only relief is found through death. Unfortunately both the snake and the hobbyist suffer needlessly: the snake physically through death, and the hobbyist mentally through feeling he has failed in his new quest.

Many times a well-meaning but ill-advised hobbyist will select a snake such as a racer or other nervous colubrid that he may have caught or have found for sale and will find that the snake is too aggressive and/or too hyperactive in his surroundings. The same may be true with some pugnacious water snakes as well. This will only serve to further discourage advanced study. This does not mean one must settle for only complacent boa constrictors. (Incidentally, I cannot recommend that boas over 4 feet in length be owned

A successful cage for snakes must imitate in a simple way the snake's natural habitat. Thus arboreal species such as this tree viper, *Bothrops schlegelii,* must have branches on which to coil. A cage need not be overly elaborate, but it must provide the snake with at least a faint "feeling of home." Photo by John T. Kellnhauser.

or handled by unaccompanied children.) One easy remedy is to read and learn your subject matter thoroughly. Further on in this book I will recommend snakes that are easily kept and lend pointers on living conditions and requirements.

One point I must make now is that under no circumstance should a beginner or amateur be allowed to keep poisonous snakes. Although many are easily kept and some are among the most beautiful and intriguing of snakes, the fact remains that they are potentially deadly and should be left to the professional herpetologist. Many communities prohibit private possession of vipers and cobras and punish offenders by fines or even imprisonment. Colubrids, species of the family Colubridae, are the "typical" snakes, make up 75% of all snake species found in North America, and include many good pets. The relatively few species of the family Boidae, boas and pythons, are some of the most diverse and interesting snakes in the world, are commonly available for sale, and are capable of keeping any hobbyist intrigued for years.

Upon choosing a pet, whether purchased or captured, it is important to check it thoroughly. First, obtain a specimen that is alert and has a shiny and firm texture to its skin. Notice any major blemishes, abrasions, or eruptions anywhere on its body. Check for parasites of any type. Using gentle pressure behind the jaws, induce the snake to open its mouth so you can check the lining of the mouth and jaws; the tissue should appear pink or white in most cases, without sores or white spots and with no obstructions or bleeding. If you are buying a snake from a petshop or other dealer, feel at liberty to ask questions. A good petshop owner will know if the individual specimen has any peculiar habits or idiosyncrasies. Any snake breathing with its lips parted, lying stretched out on its side, or excreting blood from the vent should be let go (if collected) or not purchased.

WHAT ABOUT POISONOUS SNAKES?

To recommend captive venomous snakes to a novice ophidiophile (Greek, literally translated = "snake lover") could be likened to allowing a child to play with a loaded gun. I do not wish to demean the many who are capable of such responsibility, but rather to discourage the unwitting from the inevitable mistake that may prove fatal.

All snakes are extremely agile. Whether you are carefully handling it, cleaning its cage, or feeding it, the opportunity arises for the snake to do what it was intended for: bite. Many rattlers and elapids (cobras and their relatives) will tame to a certain degree, but their actions are unpredictable, and should you pinch or frighten them or even have

Above: *Spilotes pullatus mexicanus,* a large Central American colubrid. **Below:** *Lampropeltis zonata parvirubra,* a seldom-seen mountain kingsnake. Both these snakes are advanced colubrids and thus "typical" snakes is the usual sense of the word. Photo above by John T. Kellnhauser; photo below by Bertrand E. Baur.

Above: *Trimorphodon lambda,* the Sonora lyre snake, is a nocturnal rear-fanged colubrid of southwestern American deserts and plains. Although venomous, its bite probably could not even inconvenience an adult human. **Below:** Close-up of the head of a copperhead, *Agkistrodon contortrix,* a common crotalid viper of the eastern U.S. Although venomous, copperheads seldom cause human fatalities. Photo above by Ken Lucas at Steinhart Aquarium; photo below by Jeff Gee.

the smell of food on your person (mice especially), they may strike. Even the most seasoned herpetologists have succumbed to accidental bites. I can attest to the fact (from personal experience) that while the initial bite itself will be as insignificant as a pinprick, the later effects will be excruciating. Even if treatment for the bite is successfully administered, cardiac arrest or nerve dysfunction may still result in death, and serious scarring or even less of limbs is common.

Up to the time of writing this book, I have been bitten (envenomated) twice. In 1980 I was bitten by a sidewinder (*Crotalus cerastes*) during a cage transfer incident and nearly died. In late 1981 I was bitten by a red diamondback (*Crotalus ruber*). Both accidents were due to misjudgments on my part and need not have ever happened. It is the amateur handler who never encounters poisonous snakes or the herpetologist who goes without a bite who is the true professional.

Why then do I take the time and effort to write about such species? Knowledge. These snakes do exist, and you should be aware of them and their characteristics. Poisonous snakes are recognizable on sight, but there are no infallible characters that distinguish all poisonous species from all harmless species. Pit vipers and true vipers usually have vertical pupils, a very broad head that may look arrowhead-like, and usually keeled scales; pit vipers of course have the pit between the eye and nostril. Elapids seldom have any of these characters and look like many harmless species, so it becomes necessary to recognize a cobra, krait, or coral snake on sight from experience. If you ever happen to encounter a supposedly poisonous snake, either by accident or with intent, and are unsure of its identity, leave it strictly alone.

Although few poisonous snake bites result in death, they do cause great inconvenience and suffering and may result in permanent disfigurement and other health problems. It is worth mentioning again that many communities prohibit the private possession of venomous snakes entirely.

I am often asked why the poisonous snakes exist at all. To answer this, one must examine evolution itself. Basically, the snakes developed venom out of the need to subdue prey. Poison is highly modified saliva. There are three types of venom injection systems.

The oldest and least developed (evolutionarily speaking) belongs to a few genera of the family Colubridae. Although this is generally accepted to be a non-poisonous (aglyphic) family, some genera possess grooved back teeth in the upper jaw (opisthoglyphic). Only by breaking the skin of the victim and subsequently "chewing" for several minutes can significant amounts of venom be introduced. Though bites are rare even when provoked, death has resulted from the bites of boomslangs and bird snakes, both African genera.

Next we have the proteroglyphic snakes. Made up mostly of the family Elapidae, they contain paired hollow fangs fixed toward the front of their upper maxillae. These are hypodermic-like fangs that are connected directly to the venom glands and are deeply grooved and almost immovable. Examples of such snakes are the cobras and the mambas. Venom from these snakes is usually neurotoxic, affecting the nervous system. The poison is lethal in minute quantities and will affect motor sensory functions and breathing. The onset of death is painful and often quick.

Most highly developed are the solenoglyphic snakes. This group includes the rattlers and other pit vipers and the Old World vipers belonging to the family Viperidae. These snakes have curved, hollow, movable fangs that fit neatly into muscular folds in the upper jaw. The venom is pumped by contraction from glands just behind and below the eye through ducts to the hollow fangs. If a fang breaks, as they do on occasion, replacement by another follows quickly. Viper venom is usually hemotoxic in effect, working on the red blood cells and smooth muscle, including the heart. The poison also contains an agent that readily induces widespread tissue degeneration. Basically, the red blood cells are invaded by this foreign protein and burst, so in reality the victim hemorrhages to death. Immunity to poisonous bites is passive. Only by regular medically approved injections can the effects be kept from reappearing. Even after several bites immunity cannot be built, and I might add that the injections to build immunity are costly. Also, this type of poison cannot only be fatal but can produce severe scars and permanent tissue damage to the affected area. Species like the tropical rattler (*Crotalus terrificus*) and some *C. durissus* subspecies have a venom containing a combination of hemotoxic and neurotoxic factors for which no exact antivenin is available.

The Elapidae has about 65 genera and 250 species in the family. This includes the kraits, mambas, and cobras, among others. In the Americas the coral snakes, genera *Micrurus* and *Micruroides*, belong to this family. A coral snake, *Micrurus fulvius*, is common in the southern U.S., while the only species of *Micruroides* enters Arizona from Mexico. As mentioned, these snakes have neurotoxic venom that is especially effective in subduing cold-blooded prey (other snakes and lizards) but also works well on mammals. Beautiful but deadly, they usually prefer to burrow during the day and hunt in the evening.

Three venomous species. **Above:** *Naja haja*, the Egyptian cobra, is a characteristic Old World viper; cobras are just vipers that can spread a hood. **Below:** The western rattlesnake, *Crotalus viridis*, is a widely distributed species with many distinctively colored subspecies. **Facing page:** Close-up of the head of a green mamba, *Dendroaspis angusticeps*, a rear-fanged colubrid that is often fatally venomous to humans. Photo above by Ken Lucas at Steinhart Aquarium.

The vipers comprise three subfamilies, Crotalinae, Viperinae, and Azemiopinae. The pit vipers (Crotalinae) are found chiefly in the New World (but there are some Old World species), and the other two subfamilies are restricted to the Old World. Of the about 20 genera and 200 species, there are about as many true vipers as pit vipers. Most species of Crotalinae and Viperinae are nocturnal, and most give live birth except the bushmaster (*Lachesis muta*) of South America and several Old World *Agkistrodon* and *Trimeresurus* species that lay eggs. Two groups of pit vipers, the moccasins and rattlesnakes, are found throughout the U.S. The moccasins of the genus *Agkistrodon* have two species occurring in the U.S.: *Agkistrodon piscivorus*, the cottonmouth water moccasin, and *Agkistrodon contortrix*, the copperhead. Rattlesnakes are comprised of two genera: *Crotalus*, with about 28 species, 13 in the U.S., and *Sistrurus*, with three species, two in the U.S. With very few exceptions, rattlesnakes are readily recognized by the rattle at the end of the tail that produces the typical buzzing sound when vibrated by an excited snake.

Above: *Agkistrodon acutus,* an Asian pit viper with an unusual snout.
Below: An excellently marked specimen of the cottonmouth water moccasin, *Agkistrodon piscivorus,* a seriously venomous species of the southern U.S. Photo above courtesy R. E. Kuntz.

Above: A European viper, *Vipera berus,* with part of her brood. Below: A timber rattlesnake, *Crotalus horridus,* the only large rattlesnake in the northeastern U.S. Unlike most other rattlesnakes, there is no stripe on the side of the head from the eye to the corner of the mouth.

Most members of the poisonous families are shy and will avoid confrontations. Many may not even attempt to strike unless thoroughly excited. Others, such as the cobras and the large rattlers, show cunning and intelligence that, combined with their physical prowess, make them extremely dangerous adversaries. In reality, more people in the U.S. will die during the year from dog bites or rabid animal attacks than from snakebite, but unfortunately society seems to attach a discriminatory stigma to reptiles, especially snakes, while little or none of this stigma burdens potentially harmful mammals, such as dogs or cats. Unless you are a snake handler or hunter, your chances of being struck by lightning are far greater than of being bitten by a poisonous snake.

The professionals who keep and observe venomous snakes realize that the accurate striking distance of most species is approximately one-third the body length (but over half in some species). These men and women also know that the snakes are capable of striking from virtually any position and thus use specially designed equipment for handling the snakes. Strict adherence to the creed to treat the animal with the respect it deserves has enabled us to study them closely in captivity and to experiment with their toxins as possible treatments for several ailments that plague man.

Snake Care

HOUSING

It would be unfair of me to recommend any single type of snake cage. The possibilities are vast. One hobbyist will be successful with one kind and someone else with another. Your snake's cage will not have to be elaborate. Just as in almost all other types of endeavors, you may opt for simple and inexpensive cages or fancy and costly habitats. In any case, your serpentarium does not have to be dank and drab either. You can use your own judgment, but remember that the cage must meet several standards and contain certain required features.

Relative to their body length, snakes do not require a large cage. For small varieties, such as those 18 to 24 inches long, a 10- or 15-gallon terrarium will suffice. If you plan to house a boa or python, take into consideration that the 18-inch juvenile you have now may in a few short years be 8 to 10 feet long.

Having the knowledge to construct your own cage will tend to involve you deeper in your hobby, not to mention that it may be more economical. Sturdy wooden cages with sliding glass fronts can be easy to make and can be built to your exact specifications. However, if you are like most keepers, you will find glass aquaria, obtainable at any petshop, will serve you efficiently as serpentaria. Bear in mind that abrasive materials such as metal screening or unfinished wood may lead to snout scrapes or splinters, resulting in possible infection. Some petshops now have available specially designed cages for snakes.

Whether you build or buy, please give consideration to the following. The cage should be easy to clean. If the unit is too heavy, elaborate, or badly designed, cleaning will require more work than it's worth. The cage must provide proper ventilation and an adequate view. The need for ventilation is obvious, but the view is often overlooked. While your snake's sight is not highly developed and will not require constant visual stimuli, this by no means should be taken to mean that you should isolate your snake and keep it in a box or totally shielded container. This type of treatment would constitute cruelty. Also, make sure that your snake can not get out and that unwanted people, especially children, can not get in. Snakes are agile and sensitive to their surroundings, and no matter how long they have been in captivity a loose top or small opening presents the opportunity for escape. Be sure the cage is out of reach of children and, in the case of poisonous snakes, that it is locked and out of the grasp of *any* unauthorized persons.

Pseustes sulphureus, a seldom-seen South American colubrid that rarely appears in the commercial pet market. Purchasing poorly known snakes is usually a risky business as it is difficult to determine what are the proper diet and habitat requirements. Photo by John T. Kellnhauser.

Cage decorations such as plants or scenic backgrounds are all unnecessary and will only subtract from the snake's usable space. I strongly recommend the use of a hiding box of wood or cardboard. A shoe box, folded newspaper, or similar material also will provide an area to which your snake will retreat for privacy. Give climbing material to arboreal snakes. Vine snakes, green tree pythons, and many others will prefer to eat, drink, and live 99% of the time suspended, rarely descending to the floor. Lengths of branches (scalded to remove unwanted insect life under the bark) are excellent and easy to obtain. For floor covering I suggest using old towels. They work wonderfully. Keep two or three as spares, with one in use. Fold the towel neatly so it will lie properly, then place on it the water dish (soaking dish and climbing stick if applicable) and hiding box. When the snake defecates, the other objects can be easily removed and the towel containing the feces and semi-solid block of uric acid can be removed for washing. Simply replace it with another. The folded towel also serves as an additional hiding area, with the snake retreating occasionally between the folds. If such material is unavailable for use as a substrate, you may use newspaper. Most professionals and hobbyists who house snakes in quantity will resort to newspaper. Newspaper presents no harm, deters bacterial

Species belonging to the same genus usually have similar requirements in captivity. Thus the familiar hognose snake is a toad-eater, as is the rarer southern hognose, *Heterdon simus*, shown above. The use of wood chips as a cage substrate, by the way, would disturb many keepers as wood chips have a reputation for being very hard to clean. Photo by John T. Kellnhauser.

36

growth, and is inexpensive and easily obtainable. I do not recommend sand or pebbles. Sand can be very messy and is an excellent medium for harboring bacteria, molds, and parasites.

Light and heat are important. Ultraviolet light is necessary for lizards and turtles to help stimulate vitamin production, but it is not needed for snakes. Aquarium reflectors are commonly used and help provide both heat and light. They also do a good job of adding extra weight to existing fitted wire mesh tops, and they also may be purchased as a complete custom-fitted unit. It's also useful to stick liquid crystal thermometer strips to the glass or hang a thermometer in the cage. This and keeping the cage away from windows and various drafty areas will aid in maintaining constant optimum temperatures. In the beginning you will have to experiment with bulb wattage. Any combination of up to 75 watts total is recommended. Avoid temperature extremes and try to maintain steady warmth between 78 and 85°F. You may wish to follow daily photoperiods throughout the year or maintain lighting 10 to 15 hours per day. When constant heat is necessary there would be no adverse effects to leaving the lights on continually. A relatively new product that works well in providing additional heat is a "hot rock," a formed base with an electrical heating element. Snakes find comfort in coiling around the unit and remaining until sufficiently warmed.

This *Bothrops lateralis*, a tree viper, can survive very well in a warm cage with minimal furnishings: a branch for climbing and resting upon and a water dish to provide drinking water, increase cage humidity, and make shedding easier. Photo by John T. Kellnhauser.

Water and soaking dishes should be provided at all times. Purchase a heavy dish with a flat bottom; a heavy weighted plastic one will work well. Without adequate weight you will have constant spillage accidents. The soaking dish should be larger than the drinking dish, and it too should be weighted. Both will help provide cage humidity, but a watchful eye should be kept on the amount of time your snake spends soaking. Prolonged soaking may cause ventral blister formation.

CLEANING AND HYGIENE

Snakes are good swimmers, and, although it is not necessary, providing your snake with a bath every other month is a good idea. This will help loosen the skin before shedding. It also will help dislodge any fecal particles clinging unnoticed to the vent. You can accomplish this in a household sink or tub, or if you find this objectionable, use a large pan or ice cooler. Use only fresh, warm water and never add soap or detergents.

If you make cleanliness your top priority, diseases likely will be unknown in your cage. Clean your snake's cage regularly whether it appears to need it or not. Remove feces immediately whether it is deposited by the snake or by live food. The water bowl should be scrubbed and replenished daily.

FEEDING

Snakes, as with all predators, are uniquely adapted for their lifestyle. Whether it be special coloration for camouflage or structures such as fangs, snakes are a marvel in the realm of feeding. Once the snake is removed from the wild and placed in captivity, natural feeding habits must be emulated closely, for the best sign of the snake's acceptance of its new environment will be for it to feed at regular intervals.

Without exception, snakes are carnivorous. Even so, there is great diversity among the species, and a wide range of foods is eaten. Also, juveniles and adults of the same species may have different food preferences. A snake will eat what is correct for it or it will not eat at all. Thought must be given to your snake's menu. For the beginning hobbyist, acquiring a snake that will feed on mice or rats as opposed to invertebrates, fishes, or other exotic foods may have distinct advantages. Before obtaining your pet, make sure an adequate food supply can be obtained all year round. Snakes such as the African egg-eater (*Dasypeltis scaber*) that subsists only on small bird eggs, some species of American water snake (*Nerodia*) that prefer fish, and South American vine snakes (*Oxybelis*) that favor lizards, to name

Plastic shoeboxes can serve many functions in furnishing snake cages. In the photo above are several recent hatchlings of the common kingsnake, *Lampropeltis getulus getulus.* The eggs were maintained in this shoebox, which will be the home of the hatchlings for a few more days until they start feeding. The Sinaloan milk snake shown below (a subspecies of *Lampropeltis triangulum*) is in a rather elaborate cage that features a plastic shoebox filled with moist moss to provide both cover and a possible egglaying site. Photos by Jeff Gee.

38

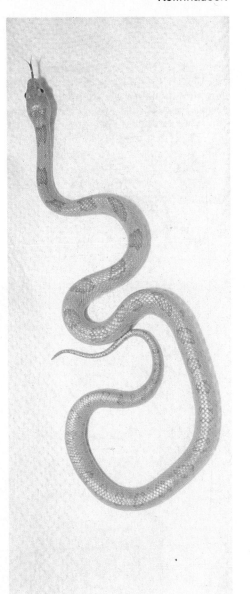

This weakly patterned snake is a juvenile Everglades rat snake, *Elaphe obsoleta rossalleni.* As the snake grows the body will become suffused with bright orange, the faint blotches will disappear, and there will develop a faint pattern of narrow stripes. Although it reaches over 7 feet in length, its color makes this a very desirable snake. Photo by John T. Kellnhauser.

just a few, are difficult at best even for the experts. If a snake's natural food is not regularly obtainable and affordable, it is best to pass that snake by.

The serious hobbyist may wish to raise his own snake food. Mice can be raised successfully with a minimum of care, but the proper type of facilities and constant cleanliness are a must. Mice require cages, special food, bedding, and other sundries. Large groups of mice tend to emit an annoying odor no matter how well maintained. Unless properly prepared, you may wish to purchase your mice (live or frozen) from a local petshop that caters to snake people. Crickets are taken by some snakes and can be purchased or raised. Water snakes often eat goldfish or even frozen smelt from the supermarket.

In captivity many snakes will accept freshly killed food or food that has been previously frozen and then thawed. Refrigerated food reserves are advantageous when an adequate food supply is unobtainable or as a matter of economy in the event live food is ignored and housing for live prey animals is unavailable. Freshly killed items may be injected in the body cavity with liquid vitamins as a supplement. Frozen or fresh-killed foods appear to be an asset to most keepers, but some experts disagree, claiming that arousal from the kill begins a series of predigestive processes that are vital to the complete digestive cycle of the snake. In any case, it has been my personal experience that many of my own captives have lived full and long lives on either pre-killed food or a mixture of live and dead foods with no obvious ill-effects.

Size and age of your snake will also be factors in feeding. A typical juvenile snake might only be able to consume "pinkie" mice, or its diet may be totally different from adults of the species. As with most growing animals, its appetite will be voracious. Adults of most rodent-eating snakes will have no problems with subduing and consuming adult mice. Large boids of course will require rats and chickens instead of mice and chicks. It is also worth mentioning that variety should be offered. It is wise to change diet as often as possible and instead of mice, for instance, offer an occasional gerbil or hamster. This will help to simulate food variety that would be normally encountered in the wild. When available, baby chicks and ducklings will be taken readily by many snakes that feed on warm-blooded prey.

Even when the proper food is offered to a particular snake, other conditions in the cage also must be stable in order to ensure that the snake will continue eating. After sufficient time has passed for the snake to become accustomed to its new environment, food may be introduced.

This acclimation period may take anywhere from three days to a week depending upon how well the snake is suited to his new conditions and when it last ate. Keeping outside distractions from interrupting and frightening the snake will reduce its timidity. A shy or frightened snake sometimes reverts to a highly agitated state and will not feed. One good idea is to provide a retreat box for your pet. Some snakes prefer using the element of surprise to attack unwary prey, and a hiding box serves well for such an ambush. Your pet may use the box for both feeding and sleeping. The box can be as simple as an inverted shoe box with a small hole cut so the snake can gain entrance or it can be specially made from plywood. A mouse placed in the cage will invariably investigate the opening of the box within a few minutes of being put into the cage.

Because snakes are cold-blooded, the optimum temperature range must be provided at all times, especially during and after feeding. When snakes are housed at lower than acceptable temperatures they may continue to feed, but they will regurgitate the partially digested bolus (lump of food) within a few days of the initial feeding. Some specimens may go off their food completely. Stable temperatures for snakes in captivity are generally between 78° and 85°F. Of course, tropical snakes may require a hot spot kept at nearly 90°F, and snakes from cooler regions may need decidedly less warmth. Nevertheless, the amount of temperature variation in the cage must be carefully controlled. Night temperatures may be eight to ten degrees cooler than day temperatures.

In addition to providing the proper food and temperature, many hobbyists will obtain specimens of snakes that are adapted to hibernating during at least part of the winter. With the onset of winter, the decision must be made as to whether you wish to skip this hibernation period or to simulate it, possibly for breeding purposes. Optimum temperature ranges may be maintained along with correct photoperiods (simulated day and evening) throughout the year with no ill-effects, and snakes usually will not hibernate if the temperature is high and food is available. However, if you do consider allowing the snake to hibernate, you must consider the requirements of the particular species. Gradually lower the temperature to about 40°. Food must not be offered directly before the hibernation period, and the specimen's colon must be completely voided before the temperature drops. Feces and undigested food in the gut may lead to enteritis and possibly death.

Feeding schedules will vary from snake to snake, depending on species, size, and type of prey. Most snakes will feed every four to six days and possibly sooner if given the op-

Only two or three foreign snakes are commonly found for sale in American pet shops, and these are almost all boas. The juvenile rainbow boa shown above (*Epicrates cenchria*) is seen much less commonly than small and half-grown common boa constrictors (*Boa constrictor*—an unusual incidence of the scientific and common names being exactly alike). Both species enter the market from tropical America. Photo above by Dr. Marcos A. Freiberg; photo below by J. K. Langhammer.

Elaphe subocularis, the Trans-Pecos rat snake, is a relatively rare snake found mostly in western Texas. At one time it was considered so rare that every specimen collected was written-up in the scientific journals, but as its range and habitat requirements became better known it was possible to collect it with regularity. Now it is considered such a prize that its collection is controlled to some extent to prevent it from being too greatly reduced in numbers. Photo by Ken Lucas at Steinhart Aquarium.

portunity. Larger snakes such as boas and pythons may only require feeding every week or two. Snakes that feed on rodents and birds tend to have slower metabolisms than those that feed on fishes, worms, and lizards. Gauging your pet's digestion rate by determining the period between eating and defecating (usually no more than 14 to 20 days) will aid you in maintaining the proper feeding cycle.

Handling the snake should be avoided for several hours after it feeds to prevent regurgitation or injury and to promote good digestion. Never handle your pet after handling its food. A snake's olfactory sense is far more acute than ours, and it may perceive the smell emanating from your hands as prey and strike. This can be painful with a boid or other species with sharp teeth.

Problems may arise when two or more snakes are housed in the same cage. Careful observation is necessary to ensure that each snake is receiving a fair share of food and that no one snake dominates or monopolizes the majority of the food. Separate feeding tanks may be utilized for well acclimated snakes. Staggered feeding days for each snake also will help stave off such problems. Also keep in mind the fact that snakes such as the mussurana (*Clelia*) and the kingsnakes (*Lampropeltis*) are usually cannibals, and keeping these with smaller species may lead to loss of the small specimens. Two snakes may also try to eat the same food, with one accidentally engesting the other. When this happens, place a cotton swab dipped in ammonia or lighter fluid near the nostrils. This will make one of the snakes let go, and it is not harmful.

Little is known about the complete eating habits of snakes. Many species have rarely been kept for any length of time due to lack of exact understanding of their full needs. Periodically snakes will go off their feed or tend to become "irregular" in feeding. This is not always cause for alarm, as it may be caused by many conditions, some serious, some not. As they reach sexual maturity, snakes will not accept food as often as they did as juveniles. Females will tend to stop feeding several weeks before laying their eggs and may not accept food for some time after laying. Also, the period during shedding may be a time of refusal. The important point is to let your snake be the judge of its requirements. If it persists in not eating for a long period of time and displays visible signs of malnutrition, your pet may be suffering from a digestive tract or respiratory ailment.

When a snake has become too weak from lack of food or illness to feed naturally, it becomes necessary to force-feed. This must be done slowly and carefully. Lean meat (no fat) and other high-protein foods are blended well with a raw egg and water for a smooth, liquid consistency that can be passed easily through a sturdy but flexible piece of narrow plastic tubing. This tube is provided at one end with a funnel and the other end is carefully inserted into the esophagus of the restrained snake, making sure the tube goes into the esophagus, not the lung. The liquid food mixture is then slowly poured into the tube, using only a small amount at a time and making sure it is really going into the snake's digestive tract. The food mixture combined with proper medication (when necessary) has proven successful on many snakes.

Don't leave mice or rats in a cage with your pet, regardless of size, for a long period of time, and *never* overnight. If a snake is not hungry and refuses to eat, it will ignore the mouse. Mice and rats soon lose their initial nervousness and may turn the tables, attacking the sleeping snake. Even snakes such as large boas and rattlers have been fatally "chewed."

Liquid multivitamins can be added to the snake's water or may be injected directly into the intended food. Only two or three drops are necessary.

One final thought on the subject of feeding. You have found out what snakes eat, when they eat, and what amounts are correct for feeding, but up to this point it has not been discussed just how they accomplish the act. With only a few exceptions, snakes swallow their prey head-first. After it has subdued its victim by whatever means employed (bites, constriction), the snake then uses its protrusible tongue to "flick" the air and locate the head of the prey. The intended prey is usually swallowed head-first because in this way its limbs will fold back out of the way to permit easier engestion. I have on occasion seen snakes that

Above: *Sonora aemula* is a rare but colorful burrowing species from the deserts of northern Mexico. The presence of the very similar black and white pattern on both the head and at midbody is intriguing. **Below:** Once considered the only American python, the Mexican *Loxocemus bicolor* is now considered to be a type of Boidae that is neither quite a boa nor a python in the normal sense. Photo above by Ken Lucas at Steinhart Aquarium; photo below by Dr. Sherman A. Minton.

The facilities to breed mice or a budget that allows the keeper to purchase mice is a must when keeping many of the most popular snakes. Whether obscure species of boas, such as the *Epicrates striatus* above, or the spectacularly colored kingsnakes, such as *Lampropeltis pyromelana* shown below, mice are a staple in the diet of many snakes. Although some specimens can be trained to take frozen and thawed mice, many will touch nothing but the living item; some snakes will only take pinkies, newly born mice. Photo above by John T. Kellnhauser; photo below by Bertrand E. Baur.

always swallowed prey tail-first. Such was the case of a southern copperhead (*Agkistrodon contortrix*) that I had a few years ago. I'm sure you must realize that in this case swallowing was accomplished only with a degree of difficulty. Nevertheless, the snake remained healthy and retained a good appetite.

Ninety-nine times out of a hundred your snake will eat using the head-to-tail method, but if on occasion it does not, there is no need for alarm. In either case, once the prey has been killed the snake will approach it while opening its mouth and distending its jaws. Jaw ligaments capable of great extension allow passage of food much larger than the head. The food is then "walked" in by moving first one side of the jaw then the other, the hooked teeth pulling the food ever further into the snake's body. Once in the mouth, secretions will begin to aid digestion and help to ease the animal on its way. On reaching the opening of the esophagus, strong muscle contractions push the food toward the stomach. The opening to the glottis (top of respiratory tract) is protrusible and slips under the prey so the snake can breathe while swallowing.

EQUIPMENT

Little will be needed in the way of additional equipment that has not already been mentioned. If you decide to gather your own snakes by collecting them yourself, it is wise to obtain collecting bags. These may be purchased, but I find that pillow cases work fine. However, if you collect poisonous specimens, never tie the collecting bag to your belt. The snake has the power and intuition to bite through the bag and into your leg. Never leave specimen bags with snakes in a closed vehicle or in direct sunlight; over-heating will cause certain death.

Most harmless snakes will bite in self-defense. These bites can be painful but prove to be of little consequence (a little alcohol and iodine will prevent infection). To avoid this, Pilstrom tongs, a pole-noose combination, or a telescopic "L" hook (baggage hook) may be employed for assistance in catching and handling snakes. These can be purchased at some petshops or through mail order dealers and will cost anywhere between $15 and $50.

It is always wise to keep on hand such items as additional aquarium lights, screen tops, and hiding boxes. Keeping the above items in stock and one or two extra holding tanks in case of accidents or unexpected new specimen additions will ensure readiness when the need arises.

One last thing—affixing to your snake cage a label with the Latin genus and species names of your snake seems to lend an air of professionalism to your hobby.

Breeding

A practice that is becoming more prevalent among pet-shop owners, herpetological clubs, and traders is the selling of sexed and matable pairs. In my opinion this action is to be commended. For all too long the hobbyist has ignored the possibility of breeding his snakes. This may be due partly to the time involved or from the fear of being incapable of handling the responsibility. Presently, it is becoming more and more important for the hobbyist to take on the added task of conservation. We are now faced with species depletion not only due to destruction of habitat but to over-collecting as well. Many species once considered to be abundant and common are now beginning to decrease in numbers, some at an alarming rate. Therefore, it is my hope that you will attempt snake breeding during the course of your hobby. It can be accomplished through a little self-sacrifice and will prove to be educational as well as beneficial. If you own one sex of a species and not the other, advertising for a mate in your local herpetological bulletin or simple outdoor scouting may be possible solutions to the problem. Ordinarily snakes will mate in the spring, but this may vary considerably depending upon the species and the amount of time the snake has been in captivity. There are seldom any obvious physical characteristics such as color to distinguish males and females of a snake species. While in lizards the courtship is usually dependent upon recognition of color and manner of display, in snakes a female will produce a distinctive (to male snakes) odor and leave a scent trail that hopefully will attract a prospective mate. When by chance this is detected, the male will follow the scent by sense of smell, rapidly flicking the tongue in and out and sorting the information through the Jacobson's organ. When the two snakes locate each other and if they are both physiologically prepared for breeding, courtship behavior will ensue. This may be as elaborate as a graceful dance with heads held high and chin rubbing lasting several minutes, or it may commence with the two entwining with little or no other movement. The actual process of mating usually lasts several hours, with the male assuming a dominate role and on occasion grasping the female with his mouth. The snakes separate after mating, and the male may breed with other females during the season.

In most common species, with the exception of the pythons, king cobra, and perhaps a few other species, once the eggs are laid or the snakelets are born there is no parental rearing or attachment. As mentioned, brooding and

Breeding snakes in captivity was once a rare event, but today keepers succeed with many species. Garter snakes have been raised through many generations in captivity, but even more successful in an economic and ecological sense is the captive breeding success with the Mexican kingsnake, *Lampropeltis mexicana.* The several subspecies or color forms of this species are rarely collected in their arid, rocky habitats in western Texas and northern Mexico, but their gorgeous color patterns of red, black, and gray have made them very popular with collectors, specimens fetching very high prices. As captive breeding of this species progresses, the snakes will become more readily available, the prices will go down, and the chances of over-collecting or perhaps even exterminating the small natural populations will disappear. Photo by R. W. Applegate.

nesting behavior are found in some species of python and may occur among a few colubrids and even a pit viper species. King cobras build nests and may be very protective of their clutch. Such behavior is limited and generally uncharacteristic of most snakes.

Snakes generally reproduce every year or every other year. Once impregnated, females can retain active sperm and may become gravid for several more seasons without additional copulation.

It is again important to bring up the point about duplicating closely the requirements of individual snakes in captivity. Accurate duplication or at least successful substitution of temperatures, foods, and hiding places is a must if the snake is to remain comfortable in its living quarters and reproduce. Following natural hibernation schedules and duplicating daily photoperiods will help to induce seasonal breeding. Males and females of about the same size can be kept together all year. Even with this continual potential to breed, many snakes become quiescent and "cage lazy," leading to lack of interest in breeding.

Should you obtain snakes that are not sexed, you can usually tell the sexes apart by careful visual comparison once you have some experience. A male will generally be distinguishable by having a longer tail than in the female, with a more gradual taper and distinctly thicker appearance at its base just behind the cloacal opening (the thicker appearance is due to the presence of the hemipenes). Determination of sex may also be made by probing behind the vent using a sterile, blunt probe prepared by spreading on it a small amount of petroleum jelly. Gently enter the rear edge of the vent so the probe passes into a small pouch (one on each side of the vent). In the male the pouch is deep and the probe penetrates easily, while in the female the pouch is a very shallow scent gland.

The sex organs of male snakes are the hemipenes, actually a single copulatory organ divided into two almost identical halves. Normally they are retracted into the pouch on each side of the cloaca, but when the male is aroused they become engorged with blood and erect themselves, projecting through the back wall of the cloaca. On the surface of the hemipenes are pleats, grooves, or spines that assist in keeping them in place in the female's oviduct during copulation. In most male snakes only the left or right hemipenis is used or favored for use in all matings, even though both are functional and capable of being used.

It is obvious that in the case of ovoviviparous snakes no special preparation by the hobbyist will be needed. Only when housing some cannibalistic species does it become necessary to immediately separate the young from the

Sexing a corn snake, *Elaphe guttata*. In the photo above, the undersides of the tails of a female (at top) and a male (at bottom) are compared. The base of the tail in the male is usually distinctly broader and heavier because of the presence of the hemipénes. The use of special small probes (photo below) allows the keeper to check the depth of the pouches at the base of the tail; in females the pouches are just shallow scent glands, but in males they are deep and house the hemipenes. Photos by Jeff Gee.

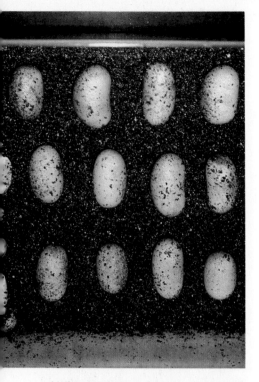

Although there are several ways of successfully hatching snake eggs, the method using vermiculite in plastic boxes is perhaps one of the most simple. Like the pie pan method described in the text, the substrate is kept slightly moist and held at about 76-80°F. Snake eggs increase considerably in size as they develop, but the shells are flexible and not easily damaged. Eggs of several species can be incubated in a single box (above), although this requires careful attention to hatching sequences of the young, or only one clutch may be kept in a box, as in the case of the indigo snake shown below. Photos by Jeff Gee.

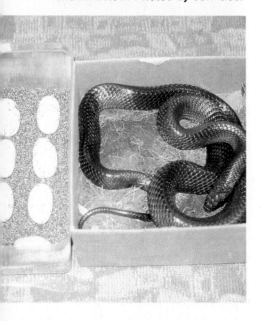

parents as soon as birth takes place to prevent the adults from eating their young. It is worth mentioning that newborn pit vipers and other poisonous snakes of all types are just as potent as their adult counterparts, allowing for their small size.

If you have an oviparous snake, a small nesting area of moist straw may be provided. Soon after the eggs are laid, remove them from the straw to prevent fungusing. In most common snakes the female will lay from about four to a dozen elongate whitish eggs. With proper care all can be hatched. Place the eggs in a dish covered with a damp towel (a metal pie pan with air holes in the bottom works perfectly). Then place another pan of the same type on top. Be careful not to jar the eggs or rest anything on top of them except for an additional damp towel. The object is to keep the eggs warm and moist and to have freely flowing air. It may take anywhere from two to three months for the eggs to hatch. Complete hatching and abandonment of the egg shell may take several days.

Snakes are hatched with a small tooth (the eggtooth) attached to the middle of the upper jaw on the snout. This tooth is used for cutting the outer membrane of the egg, allowing the snake to escape. A short time after hatching, the tooth is shed or absorbed.

The young snake grows at a rapid rate, and shedding of its skin will be frequent for the first year. Depending on the type of snake, maturity usually will be attained in two to four years. As expected, in the larger snakes (boids, pythons) it takes considerably longer to reach maturity, sometimes five to six years. Growth continues throughout life but will slow greatly after maturity is reached.

There are usually obvious coloration and marking differences between juveniles and adults of many species. The juvenile patterns will change gradually until maturity, and deepening or dulling of the colors will be seen in snakes of middle and advanced age.

The main benefits to breeding have already been mentioned, and an enterprising hobbyist will soon realize the secondary advantages of captive propagation. Utilizing the new stock for additional study will open further avenues for you to gain more knowledge and expand your interests. Also, these snakes may be used for sale or trade to other herptile enthusiasts. In addition, with proper supervision a few could be returned to the geographic area from which the parents came in order to maintain the numbers of the species in the wild.

Ailments and Cures

Preventive disease maintenance in the care of your snakes is always your best bet. Using common sense and being familiar with the telltale signs of impending trouble will save you time and expense and will save your snake from serious illness. In captivity snakes are prone to far more sickness than they would encounter in their natural habitat. A snake in the wild would be able to change its living conditions or vary its diet when troubled by parasites or infection, whereas in captivity its movements and living conditions are obviously restricted. With captive snakes, the responsibility for proper living conditions and medical care rests upon the keeper.

The first step is to be sure that you are starting with a good specimen. Check any new specimen thoroughly for mites, dermal eruptions, wounds, parted lips, abnormal secretions, and any other factors that might cause trouble later on.

To elaborate upon pathological conditions of the internal organs would be beyond the scope of a book for the average hobbyist. Therefore, diseases involving mechanical trauma (injury), ectoparasites, fungi, and bacteria will be the major topics discussed. If any serious problems are suspected, immediately consult a veterinarian who treats snakes. Many times zoos will employ a staff vet who may be a specialist with reptiles, or at least they may be able to direct you to a local veterinarian who handles diseases of snakes. Time is often of importance in treatment of diseases of any animals, and snakes are no exceptions.

Any snake that is diseased must be separated from all others and placed in separate quarantine quarters. Limit such a cage to only a water dish (for drinking) and possibly a rock or climbing lattice. Provide a simple cage substrate such as a towel or piece of newspaper. Both are easily replaced and absorbent, and it is claimed that newspaper inhibits the growth of bacteria. As mentioned before, optimum temperatures must be maintained along with the correct humidity for the species. Beginners will encounter feeding and shedding problems and listless attitudes among their pets, but these are usually relatively simple problems that the proper heat and humidity will quickly correct upon adjustment. Gastrointestinal ailments and accidents involving crushing, rupturing, and fracturing will be your most serious (and sometimes fatal) problems.

This western patchnosed snake, *Salvadora hexalepis,* is finishing a shed. Notice the loose skin just behind the head and the difference in color of the head (darker, older skin) and the body (lighter, newer skin). Many problems with snakes in captivity start with poor shedding, but by maintaining the proper humidity for the species and having water bowls available many problems can be averted. Photo by Ken Lucas at Steinhart Aquarium.

SHEDDING

Molting or shedding is not considered a disease, but it can be a primary cause of complications when the shed is difficult or incomplete. Often hobbyists will maintain the correct temperature but will neglect the proper humidity. Proper humidity can be maintained by ensuring the correct moisture is found throughout your home and especially in the room where the snake is kept. Also, a water dish and a bathing dish kept clean and full daily will help ensure proper climate control. A snake will generally shed its skin completely in a short period of time (a few hours or days at most). When the humidity is incorrect, the snake may shed its skin in fragments. When this happens, if pieces of old skin are allowed to remain on the snake they may lead to skin disease due to fungal infections (mycosis) or may become an excellent hiding place for mites. To prevent this, maintain proper humidity in the cage and provide your snake with an adequate soaking dish. The large boas and pythons may require additional larger soaking dishes, and during their shedding period they can be placed in a styrofoam cooler with a top. If shedding is incomplete you may try to pull or peal off the dead layer of skin by hand. Use caution and only pull to the point where there is resistance. In a difficult shed, pulling off skin that is not really ready may result in irritation and even bleeding. Unless obviously in trouble, however, it is best to let the snake shed by itself.

Once Jeff Gee, a highly experienced herpetologist, and I encountered an unusual problem with a captive tiger rattler (*Crotalus tigris*). The snake had completed shedding to midway of its 30-inch length, when it inadvertently had been offered food. It swallowed an adult mouse, but because the snake's shed skin was tightly bunched around its midsection, the partially digested mouse could not pass any further through the gut. This caused circulatory problems, and the snake's head began to swell. Several hours passed before the snake was checked, but corrective steps were begun immediately after discovery of the problem. After subduing the rattler, we proceeded to shed the snake manually. While stripping off the bunched skin at midbody, we noticed backward movement of the lump of food almost immediately. After 15 minutes the snake's swelling decreased and activity returned to normal.

ACCIDENTS

Pet snakes frequently suffer from rough handling and neglect. Damage to the spinal column and head and serious puncture wounds may ultimately lead to death. These can be easily avoided and need never happen. One common but

Molting or shedding brings out the color of a snake, changing an often dull, brownish specimen into a glossy object of beauty. This eastern kingsnake, *Lampropeltis getulus getulus,* is about halfway through a shed. Photo by Ken Lucas at Steinhart Aquarium.

The fox snake, *Elaphe vulpina gloydi,* is found only in the midwestern U.S. and is seldom available commercially, though it makes a fairly good pet. Although water bowls are a must, some snakes may become addicted to bathing, which can result in the growth of fungus or bacteria on the skin. Photo by John T. Kellnhauser.

A large, docile snake such as an indigo snake, *Drymarchon corais*, is easy to handle as long as it is not excited, but the same specimen if irritated or frightened can be a real handful of trouble if not securely grasped. Photo courtesy American Museum of Natural History.

Snakes from dry habitats, such as this long-nosed snake, *Rhinocheilus lecontei*, from southern California, are subject to respiratory problems if the cage is kept either too cold or too humid. This greatly limits the success of keeping such snakes by beginners who have little experience in detecting the first signs of respiratory infections among their charges. Photo by Ken Lucas at Steinhart Aquarium.

surprising source of injury is bites from rodent food animals left in the cage with the snake overnight. Every keeper must learn to be cautious in leaving with a snake live mice or rats intended as food. Jeff Gee told me a story about this problem and the sale of a juvenile common boa to an inexperienced youth. A few days later the boa was returned by the distraught mother and her son. They had left a mouse in with the snake overnight in the same cage, and the snake, although alive, was now motionless and severely injured. Large, deep cuts were present, with substantial loss of blood. Mr. Gee took the snake, which was undoubtedly in a lot of pain, and managed to save its life. Using tape to secure the boa to a clean board, he then washed and dressed the wounds. Using a sterile curved needle and medium suture, he baseball-stitched the larger wounds. Upon completion of the surgery, the snake was retired to a separate cage. In two weeks it miraculously showed signs of healthy improvement. The stitches were later removed, and full recovery was gained. Today the snake remains healthy but still has the scars to bear witness to the accident. Hopefully none of your snakes will need such drastic and dramatic treatment. Use of some common sense and care should prevent most problems.

SKIN DISEASES

Fungal infections (mycosis) are noticed usually on the ventral scales of snakes. Often brown blisters containing pus will appear and, if left unchecked, will spread rapidly. To be successful, treatment must begin early. The common cause of fungal infections seems to be moist living conditions—too much bathing and a constantly damp substrate are to blame. As soon as the blisters are recognized, clean the cage and start treatment immediately. Draining the blisters and treating them with iodine and a bath in ethyl alcohol while keeping the snake warm and dry may be the only treatment necessary for recovery. For more serious cases your veterinarian may have to use antifungal drugs.

COLDS AND MINOR RESPIRATORY PROBLEMS

Viral and bacterial infections are not uncommon among snakes. If you house, transport, or acquire a snake during the winter months in cold climates, it is necessary to keep the snake at the proper temperature. A snake with a respiratory infection will tend to breathe with its head and upper body held high, and parting of the lips also may be observed. The snake will seem restless and nervous. It will not take food, and dried mucus will form around its nostrils. The lungs and nasal passages are blocked, and, as with humans, the usual amount of discomfort is present. My

wife and I successfully treated a pair of canebrake rattlers (*Crotalus horridus*) by force-feeding them with a small amount of powdered penicillin suspended in a solution of liquid multivitamins and raw egg. This was administered twice daily and proved to be a cure in 15 days. As a guard against infections, water-soluble broad-spectrum antibiotics may be purchased and added in small amounts to your snake's water supply. Although this may be effective in keeping the snake's condition strong, many people believe that overuse of broad-spectrum antibiotics allows bacteria to develop immunity to common drugs, thus making future treatment more difficult.

Milk snakes are several species and subspecies of kingsnakes that have distinctive banded patterns of red, black, and yellow, white, or orange. They are among the most sought-after snakes. Although they are expensive, they usually adapt well to captivity and live long lives. However, because they require live foods that must be cultured (such as mice and lizards) beginners should not try them until experienced with less expensive snakes. Photo by Jeff Gee of the Honduran subspecies of *Lampropeltis triangulum*.

INTESTINAL COMPACTION

All snakes, without exception, require exercise or intestinal upset comparable to constipation can result. The abdomen becomes distended and tight, and the snake may become reluctant to move or may prefer to roll on its side or

The mangrove snakes are sometimes available commercially, but they are not for beginners. They are expensive, mildly venomous, and require tropical habitats. This is the pale phase of *Boiga irregularis.* Notice the enlarged scales along the midline of the back that are typical of the genus. Photo by John T. Kellnhauser.

back. Usually blamed for this condition is the buildup of a block of solid uric acid in the vent. Generally, careful massage will help this pass. If clotted blood is found in the passed stool, ulcerations or other internal disorders may be present, and diagnosis and treatment by a veterinarian will be necessary.

STARVATION

Long-term failure to eat in captivity will produce a host of problems, and some specimens will die in a relatively short period of time from simple starvation. Such starved animals have the usual thin, desiccated appearance typical of any starved animal. In other cases snakes may live for long periods of time with little or no feeding but will succumb to the lowered resistance and general systemic breakdown brought out by malnutrition. Death soon follows due to other pathological factors, such as mouth rot, ulcerations, atrophy of the intestines, pneumonia, and endocarditis in any combination.

Some of the causes relating to this may be unpleasant housing conditions, excessive handling, irregular feeding schedules, constant moving, or abrupt changes. If the snake does not feed and no other remedy is offered, let the snake go free in its natural habitat or give the snake to an experienced handler who might have better luck.

MOUTH ROT

A rare but highly contagious and hard to get rid of disease, mouth rot is characterized by patchy white spots on the gums and a foul smell caused by bacteria of the genus *Pseudomonas.* The lining of the mouth is affected, and in advanced cases the teeth may be missing or soft. Generally snakes having mouth rot are those that have been neglected for quite sometime. Many will display symptoms of other diseases as well. Treatment should include a broad-spectrum antibiotic and cleansing of the infected area with an aqueous solution of sulfamethiazine. Adding vitamins to the food is important and will help replace some of the nutrients lost due to the inability to eat. Healing and regeneration should be rapid.

MITES

Ectoparasites such as mites commonly plague snakes. Mites are tiny arachnids no bigger than the tip of a pen. They pose no threat to humans (other than occasional mild irritation), but if left unchecked large populations can kill a snake in a matter of days. Mites are blood-suckers that reproduce quickly. Large numbers of mites can hide under the overlapping edges of the scales and be found only on very careful examination. If your snake is infested, place it in a container of warm water and leave only the head above water. The mites will drown in a few minutes to an hour. Other cures include placing the snake in a box containing a generous amount of Dri-Die powder. This powder is a dehydrating agent to mites and their eggs, while being non-toxic to snakes. **Warning:** Commercial flea powders mixed with or containing Dri-Die are toxic to snakes and will cause death. Inquire of your pharmacist or veterinarian as to how to obtain this product. Cages that have contained contaminated snakes must be cleaned and all the contents must be destroyed or enough mites will be hidden to start a new population. A common source of infestation is natural tree branches, which can be literally crawling with mites. I suggest that artifical climbing lattices and decorations be used, and it doesn't hurt to dip the decorations in boiling water for a few minutes before adding them to the cage.

SELF-INFLICTED INJURY

As a rule, most types of racers, whipsnakes, and similarly active species make poor captive specimens. They are usually too aggressive and active to completely tame, and

A juvenile red racer, *Masticophis flagellum piceus,* from southern California. As the snake ages the blotches will be lost and the color will change to an almost solid dark reddish brown with a faintly braided pattern caused by darker scale edges. The many subspecies of *Masticophis flagellum* are often called coachwhips. Photo by Ken Lucas at Steinhart Aquarium.

Contia tenuis, the sharp-tailed snake, is found only along the mountains of the Pacific Northwest and California. It is a secretive species that is seldom collected although it can be locally common. Many keepers who have had access to this species have found it difficult to maintain. Photo by Ken Lucas at Steinhart Aquarium.

they constantly rub their snouts or bang their heads into the sides of the cage, often resulting in injury or infection. Snout abrasions may be treated like any open wound, with application of iodine or Mercurochrome. Avoid using cages with screen fronts or unfinished wooden panels that increase the chance of abrasion. If such untamable behavior continues for an extended period of time, it is best that the snake be released from captivity or transferred to a more experienced keeper who might have more luck.

INTERNAL PARASITES

Serious diseases such as amoebiasis or large populations of intestinal parasitic worms (helminths) tend to be rare, but while not always easily detected, they are often deadly. Snakes affected by very large numbers of such organisms will lack an appetite, lie on their sides, and have bloody or loose excrement with a foul smell. If noticed in their early stages, most infections from internal parasites can be controlled. The parasites are often easily transmitted to other snakes through direct contact, feces, or tainted food and water. If internal worms or other parasites are suspected, I recommend seeing a vet immediately.

Finally, I must say that most of the conditions mentioned need never be encountered by most hobbyists. Snakes are clean and healthy if kept in hygienic conditions and provided with living conditions that attempt to duplicate their natural environment and lifestyle.

Popular Choices

As a guideline to selecting "easy to keep snakes," I have prepared short comments on just a few of the many types of snakes that can be recommended as pets. There are, of course, many more harmless species that will make fine captives as well, but for the beginner's sake I have taken into account many of the most important factors that will determine one's probable success with a certain snake. These factors, such as availability of the snake and its food, how easy it is to house, its temperament, and its average size, have all been considered when selecting examples to include in this chapter.

The snakes considered in this section represent only two (Boidae and Colubridae) of the 12 or so major families of snakes. To better acquaint you with the snake families commonly recognized, a list of the families and a brief summary of each family's characters are included. Please note that many herpetologists recognize more or fewer families. Especially common is the combination of Hydrophiidae with Elapidae.

Try to make it a practice to become familiar with the scientific (Latin) names. Often the common name given to a particular snake may be ambiguous or may differ in various areas. By using the accepted scientific nomenclature there can be no mistake when talking about any species. One example is *Heterodon platyrhinos*. This common colubrid is found throughout the eastern U.S. and may be called the hognose, blow snake, puff adder, or false adder, among other names, but it has only one scientific name.

The Classification of Snakes

Kingdom Animalia— All living organisms except plants and bacteria.

Phylum Chordata— Animals with the nerve cord of the central nervous system located above the digestive system; usually a backbone is present.

Class Reptilia— Cold-blooded vertebrates that breathe through lungs, not gills, and usually have scales and claws.

Order Squamata— The lizards and snakes. Defined on internal characters of the skull and skeleton, but obviously not crocodilians or turtles.

The corn snake, *Elaphe guttata,* is widely distributed over the United States and is very variable in details of color and pattern. Western specimens are usually brownish and dull, while specimens from Florida are often brightly colored, sometimes almost solid orange with the blotches fading into the background. Additionally, juveniles tend to have darker and more distinct blotches that fade as the animal grows. This is a juvenile specimen of a northeastern population. Photo by Aaron Norman.

Suborder Serpentes—	Only snakes; no external usable legs; no eyelids or external ear opening.
Families	(Listed in approximate phylogenetic order. Snake families are defined by characters of the soft anatomy and skeleton, and their technical definition is often difficult.)
1. Typhlopidae 2. Leptotyphlopidae 3. Anomalepididae	All three of these related families are harmless burrowers confined mainly to tropical regions. Comprised of well over 200 species, they are very secretive, have dot-like eyes, and do not do well in captivity.
4. Aniliidae	South American pipesnakes; primitive burrowers with patterns like coral snakes, red and black bands.
5. Uropeltidae 6. Xenopeltidae	Two related groups commonly referred to as shieldtails and sunbeam snakes respectively. Both are burrowers from southern Asia. The shieldtails are noted for an enlarged scale or shield at the end of their tail. The sunbeam snakes are characterized by their shiny coloration and are considered by many to be related to either the colubrid or boid families.
7. Boidae	This family includes the popular boas, pythons, and anacondas. Size varies from about a foot to over 30 feet. Males usually have spurs near the vent. Many herpetologists recognize three or four different families for these snakes.
8. Acrochordidae	A small family found from Asia to Australia near the coasts. They are noted for their large tubercles, hence the common name wart snakes. The skin is exceedingly loose. They are considered by some to be a subfamily of the colubrids. Thoroughly aquatic, they lack the wide ventral scutes of typical colubrids and seem to do well in captivity.
9. Colubridae	This family represents about ¾ of all known snakes. They usually have large scales on top of their heads. Few poisonous members are found in this family, but those that are venomous have the fangs at the back

Typhlops braminus, an Asian blindsnake of the family Typhlopidae. This species has become widely distributed by stowing away in the roots of potted plants, much like earthworms. Photo courtesy of R. E. Kuntz.

The sunbeam snake, *Xenopeltis unicolor,* a unique burrowing species from Asia that is probably closest to the boas but has several characters that make it difficult to relate to other living snakes. Photo by Dr. Sherman A. Minton.

This gopher snake is the epitome of a snake in the thinking of many people. It is a colubrid, like most other North American snakes. Photo by Ken Lucas at Steinhart Aquarium.

Laticauda species, a primitive sea snake of the family Hydrophiidae. Unlike most other sea snakes, this genus has species able to move about readily on land and lays eggs on land. Photo by Bruce Carlson.

of the upper jaws. This family is almost impossible to define technically, and its many members may not all be closely related.

10. Elapidae — Included in this family are the infamous cobras, mambas, and kraits. These snakes have a chiefly neurotoxic venom, are mostly nocturnal, and have fixed hollow fangs at the front of the mouth.

11. Hydrophiidae — This poisonous family is known as the sea snakes. Most species rarely exceed two feet. They live and breed in the water, bearing living young (with one exceptional genus that lays eggs on land). Most have strongly flattened rudder-like tails.

12. Viperidae — Both the Old World vipers and the New World vipers (with the "facial pit") make up this familiar family. All are known for their stout build and toxicity. The fangs are movable. This highly evolved family contains the rattlesnakes, copperhead, tree vipers, and many other species.

FAMILY BOIDAE

The family Boidae encompasses several groups of snakes now placed in several families or subfamilies, but to the average hobbyist the broad groups of "boas" and "pythons" will suffice. Comprised of approximately 100 species, snakes of this family tend to be large and constrict their prey, which usually consists of mammals and birds. The family is restricted mainly to moist tropical forests and to semi-arid regions where temperature variance will be slight all year long. Several small species do occur among both boas and pythons, but even though they are quite interesting and attractive, they have not enjoyed the popularity of their larger kin.

General differences between pythons and boas lie in their skull structure and modes of reproduction. The difference between the skulls deals with the number of bones and their relative size and position, factors of little concern to the hobbyist. However, the boa constrictors, rainbow boas, anacondas, and their relatives produce living young, whereas the pythons lay eggs. Boas are found chiefly in the New World (though there are several Old World genera), and the pythons are found almost exclusively in the Old World (Asia, Australia, Africa). The boas and pythons typically have paired lungs, and most have pelvic girdle remnants and anal spurs. The average length for the family is probably somewhere between 8 and 12 feet, with few species under 4 feet long and only a few pythons and anacondas greatly exceeding 15 feet. Each group has one member that may attain a length of 30 feet or more: both *Python reticulatus* (reticulated python) and *Eunectes murinus* (anaconda) reach or exceed this length. Most species are of calm demeanor and do well in captivity, although some tree boas and various pythons, especially when captured wild, will bite viciously and can inflict substantial wounds. I personally have had the misfortune of turning my back on a reticulated python while standing too close and have had my neck slightly lacerated. I advise that all snakes over 20 feet in length never be handled alone and that no specimen should ever be placed at face- or eye-level. Children of course must be kept away from large boas and pythons or must be very carefully supervised by experienced adults. Large pythons have undoubtedly caused serious accidents involving small children and even adults.

Many boas and pythons make excellent pets. Food for most will be mice and rats, and all do well in proportionately small cages. Soaking and/or climbing are their favorite pastimes. The temperature should be maintained at at least 82°F, with high humidity (except for desert species).

Hatchlings and young specimens of the green tree boa, *Corallus caninus*, are bright orange to orange-brown. Only as they mature does the color gradually change to the vivid green typical of adults. Photo by J. K. Langhammer.

Above: *Tropidophis greenwayi,* a small, rare island boa from the Caribbean. The many species of this genus are poorly known and seldom seen. Some scientists believe the genus is not a true boa and deserves its own family. **Below:** *Epicrates cenchria maurus,* a subspecies of the rainbow boa in which the dorsal pattern is weak and the snake appears almost uniformly glossy brown at first glance. Photos by Dr. Sherman A. Minton.

Although it is a good idea to provide one, most boids find little use or interest in hiding boxes and prefer either to sit coiled on the floor of the cage in the open or to sit in well-elevated branches.

The average life span for most boids can be expected to be about 20 to 30 years, but inexperienced keepers have a tendency to overfeed their pets, and many die early from heart failure due to obesity. It may also be mentioned that keepers have been able to train these large snakes to defecate on paper or in water dishes, enabling the snake to be "set free," so to speak, in the house. I recommend this only when no other small pets (cats, dogs, birds) are kept. I have found that obtaining a juvenile of no more than a foot or two in length and raising it into a well-cared-for adult is the perfect learning experience. Many pythons and boas seem to mate without hesitation in captivity, and the eggs or young are relatively easy to maintain. Captive-bred stock of several species is available. Hybrids and albinos have high market values among traders, though they are often weaker than normal snakes and are more difficult to maintain.

Availability of many species of boas and pythons is now limited or even impossible due to enforcement of endangered species laws and various local laws affecting importation, sale, and possession of large snakes. Several species can no longer be imported at all, and many others require permits.

When obtaining any of these snakes there can not be any guarantee that your specimen, no matter which species, will be gentle and act tame. Among these snakes are several that can generally be expected to act in a tame manner. Unfortunately, some hobbyists find that individuals of even these species are divided as to temperament. It is not unusual to purchase a python and find it to be totally belligerent, striking at you throughout its life. If you have such a specimen or some day get a snake like this, your only problem will exist in actually handling the snake. It has been noted that possessing intractable moods does not subtract from the willingness of boas and pythons to thrive in captivity in most cases.

A good method that works effectively in training even the most vicious captives is to wear an undershirt or similar garment for two or three days. The shirt is then put in the cage with the snake and left there several days or it can be tied to a yardstick and used to gently stroke the snake near its head until you find that the snake will allow your touch. This method works on the premise that the snake will pick up your scent particles from the shirt and after a period of time should equate your odor with non-aggression. This method works not only with boids but has been proven effective with other species also by hobbyists and zoo keepers alike. The method is not fail-safe, but at any rate it is worth a try and may save you some bites. Remember that this method will only be successful when combined with an easy approach, gentle touch, and comfortable housing conditions.

BOA CONSTRICTOR *(Boa constrictor)*

Surrounded by myth and used frequently in horror shows, the common boa constrictor is the leader in petshop snake sales. Boas occur in various races from Mexico to the Amazon and into southern South America, with the lighter subspecies, especially the Colombian "red-tailed" boas, being the most docile. Most give birth in early spring (late April or May) to about 25 or more snakelets that are usually under a foot long. The babies will feed well on small mice (pinkies). Fully grown adults may reach 10 to 12 feet in length and exhibit great strength. Be cautious when purchasing specimens. Due to inadequate procedures during shipping, many of these snakes arrive ill, either with colds or with mouth rot. Before purchasing any boa, it is wise to check for any evidence of such disease.

Boa constrictors are very popular and are highly recommended species. Being more abundant than many other boas, juveniles can be obtained commercially in the spring

Above: Detail of the head of *Boa constrictor.* Contrast this with the pattern of the rainbow boa shown on the facing page at the bottom. **Below:** *Epicrates angulifer,* a tree boa from the West Indies. Although somewhat attractive and occasionally available for sale, this relative of the rainbow boa is usually vicious and nervous and seldom makes a good pet. Photo above by Dr. Marcos A. Freiberg; photo below by J. Dodd.

Above: Detail of the spur of a tree boa (*Epicrates*). Most boas have spurs, though they are usually larger in males than in females. These are vestigial remnants of the hindlegs.
Below: Detail of the head of the rainbow boa, *Epicrates cenchria.* Photo above by J. Dodd; photo below by Dr. Marcos A. Freiberg.

at moderate cost. The young grow quickly and require food (one mouse) approximately every eight to ten days. Maintain the temperature at about 82°F and provide a large water dish and a climbing lattice. Due to dwindling populations, it is suggested that if adult boa constrictors are purchased they should be obtained as a matable pair. In mature boas the sexes can be distinguished through the length of the anal spurs, with the males having spurs that are much longer and more obvious than in females. The probing method will have to be used when sexing immature boas.

RAINBOW BOA *(Epicrates cenchria)*

Also a favorite with hobbyists because of its beauty and calm demeanor, this boa's natural habitat ranges from southern Central America to Argentina. Rarely will its length exceed 6 feet. It is a ground-dwelling boa that climbs when forced to and eats a variety of warm-blooded food items, such as birds, rodents, bats, and (in nature) small deer. This boa (as well as several other boas and pythons) possesses pits on the lip scales (labials) that detect radiant heat much like the facial pit of the pit vipers. A similar species, *Epicrates striatus*, the Haitian boa, sometimes exceeds 7 feet but is plainer in coloration and frequently ill-tempered; many hobbyists report difficulty in feeding it. Other Caribbean *Epicrates* are occasionally imported, but they seldom make as interesting pets as the rainbow boa.

ROSY BOA *(Lichanura trivirgata)*
RUBBER BOA *(Charina bottae)*

The small, slow-moving rosy boa is native to the western U.S. and Mexico. It is very "blunt" in shape and easily housed in small cages. It will thrive on rodents and lives best in a dry cage provided with a "hot rock" or regular rock with an overhead light. Adults reach almost 4 feet in length. Another small northern boa is the rubber boa *(Charina bottae)* of moist mountain forests from British Columbia to California. It seldom exceeds 2 feet in length.

EMERALD TREE BOA *(Corallus caninus)*
GREEN TREE PYTHON *(Chondropython viridis)*

The emerald tree boa and its convergent python counterpart, *Chondropython viridis*, are very similar in appearance and habits even though separated by thousands of miles and being unrelated. *Corallus caninus* is from tropical South America; *Chondropython viridis* is from New Guinea. Both are rare in captivity, and even when offered commercially, hobbyists will find them expensive and generally difficult

The rarely seen Solomon Islands boa, *Candoia* species. Although certainly boas, it is not sure exactly which other boas are their closest relatives. Very few boas are found in the Pacific, where pythons are more typical. Photo by Jeff Gee.

The rubber boa of the western U.S., *Charina bottae.* This small solid brown boa is found further north than any other species of boa. Photo by Richard Haas.

64

A study in boa contrasts. Above is *Corallus caninus,* a bright green arboreal species from tropical South America. Below is *Lichanura trivirgata,* a brownish burrowing species from the deserts of western America. Photo above by Dr. Marcos A. Freiberg; photo below by Ken Lucas at Steinhart Aquarium.

to keep. These snakes have laterally compressed bodies with strongly prehensile tails and spend 95% of their time tightly coiled around branches. Both have long, curved teeth that can inflict messy bites.

In order to be successful with either species, strict duplication of the natural temperature and humidity must be provided as well as sufficient climbing material and plenty of foliage to help keep the snake obscured from direct sight. All tree boids of this type will require a variety of food items, including small birds and rodents. These species are slender and seldom reach 6 feet in length. The *Corallus* is born bright orange but gradually changes to green upon reaching maturity. Most specimens have rather bad tempers, sometimes striking at even slight movements.

Other smaller South American tree boas, such as *Corallus enydris* (the garden tree boa) and *Corallus cooki* (Cook's tree boa) are sometimes available and present similar problems, although Cook's tree boa adapts fairly well to captivity.

ANACONDA *(Eunectes murinus)*
YELLOW ANACONDA *(Eunectes notaeus)*

These are the largest of the New World snakes. When encountered in the wild, most will hiss loudly and strike. Strikes from adults are painful and can even fracture bones. Individuals inhabit waterways and feed by constricting and drowning large prey. The muted lozenges of black and yellow on green make them hard to see in the water and shadows. Long lives and unpredictable dispositions are trademarks of these giants. When offered by petshops, prices on these snakes will be substantially higher than for all other common boids. The common anaconda, *E. murinus*, is found over much of northern and central South America, while the yellow anaconda, *E. notaeus*, is found in the drier forests south of the Amazon basin. The common anaconda reaches at least 32 feet in length and is an exceedingly heavy snake at such sizes; the smaller yellow anaconda seldom exceeds 15 feet.

SAND BOAS *(Eryx species)*

These rather plain but very stout-bodied boas are unconventional pets. There are about ten species found in drier regions (even deserts) of Africa and Asia. At least two or three species are commonly imported for sale. Birds and mice are staples of their diets. A hot, dry cage with several inches of fine sand is needed, for they tend to remain buried in the sand all day. I do not recommend these for beginners but do feel compelled to mention the genus and give credit to the keepers inclined to house them.

Above: A juvenile anaconda, *Eunectes murinus*. With luck, this specimen could grow to 20 feet in length. These are aquatic boas and must have access to a swimming area such as a child's swimming pool. **Below:** *Eryx tataricus*, a sand boa. Several species of this genus reach the market from Africa and India, and they are often relatively inexpensive. They require dry, warm, habitats. Photo above by J. Dodd; photo below by Dr. Sherman A. Minton.

Above: *Liasis olivaceus,* an Australian python that at first glance looks more like a colubrid racer than a "typical" python. Below: *Python molurus molurus,* the Indian python, a subspecies now on the endangered species list and very difficult to obtain. Its more common Burmese cousin (*P. m. bivittatus*) has a distinct brown arrowhead on top of the head, while in the Indian python the arrowhead is indistinct anteriorly. Photos by Dr. Sherman A. Minton.

LARGE PYTHONS (*Python* species)

These pythons include several very large species, one even rivaling the anaconda in size. The several species are found in Africa, Southeast Asia, and Australia. They are popular with hobbyists even though many are unpredictable and aggressive. Pythons can be successfully bred in captivity, and with recent reduction in availability of several species I strongly recommend it. All are oviparous, and in most cases they incubate their clutch—the female coils about the nest and through muscle movement actually generates heat. Their appetites are large and growth to adulthood is rapid, so a sufficiently large cage must be provided to allow for this growth. Even captive-born and supposedly "tame" specimens often bite. This will not be fatal, of course, but handlers must realize that eventually you may be bitten by one species or another; this can only be accepted. Pythons require a large, sturdy soaking dish, warm temperatures, and climbing lattices for some species. The adults need correspondingly large food, such as chickens, ducks, or guinea pigs. The largest of these snakes are extremely powerful and agile, so don't underestimate their strength. Handle them only when a willing friend or "spotter" is present. Many species are becoming rare due to ex-

ploitation, and when and if they are found commercially they can be quite expensive. If offered the correct living conditions, most species make beautiful, long-lived pets.

INDIAN PYTHON (Python molurus molurus)
BURMESE PYTHON (Python molurus bivittatus)

These two closely related subspecies from India and Sri Lanka (*P. m. molurus*) and Southeast Asia (*P. m. bivittatus*) are among the largest species of the genus. The Indian, whose export is restricted, is a smaller (15 feet) and somewhat tamer version of the Burmese (23 feet). Both forms can, on occasion, be obtained through domestic breeding, but permits will be necessary for the Indian python. The Burmese python is still relatively commonly imported and presently unrestricted. Unfortunately, some individuals may hiss loudly, strike, and resent handling. Such specimens are exceptions, because many friends of mine have had Burmese pythons of 20 feet or more that have been as tame as house cats. For those of you who choose a python, only time and patience will out. Adults retain the ornate and colorful pattern scheme they presented as juveniles.

RETICULATED PYTHON (Python reticulatus)

A staple item at petshops, this particular species holds the generally accepted world record as the longest known snake: 32' 9½". Deriving its name from its woven pattern of gold, brown, and black, this beautiful snake is more successfully kept when obtained from captive-reared stock as opposed to specimens captured wild. A female can lay up to 90 or 100 eggs and will incubate them by raising her body temperature through muscle contractions. Incubation will last approximately three months, with the hatchlings being about 20 inches in length. At this size, small mice may be offered as food with no problem. Reticulated pythons have a reputation for being vicious and often untamable, although some specimens make fine pets. A 20-foot reticulated python is an extremely strong animal that must be handled with care.

BLOOD PYTHON (Python curtus)

In my opinion, this species is the most beautiful and most adaptable to captive life. This docile python rarely grows larger than 10 feet in length. It makes an exceptional pet, the only drawbacks being that it is hard to locate commercially and is very expensive.

ROCK PYTHON (Python sebae)

Indigenous to Africa, these pythons are considered to be among the really huge snakes also. Rock pythons regularly

Above: *Python reticulatus,* the reticulated python, is probably the most spectacular of the pythons, sometimes reaching over 20 feet in length. Many specimens have vicious tempers and are very unpredictable, however, and have caused human fatalities. **Below:** The carpet python, *Morelia spilotes* form *variegata,* is another unusual Australian species that is rarely seen in petshops. Photo above by H. Hansen, Aquarium Berlin; photo below by Dr. Sherman A. Minton.

grow to over 20 feet in length and can be treated much like any other large pythons. Once adulthood is reached, food need only be offered every 12 days on the average. Because of its large size, exercise caution when handling it.

BALL PYTHON (*Python regius*)

Another good-natured and easily kept python, these snakes rarely attain 5 feet. Recent captives of this species and the burrowing python (*Calabaria reinhardtii*) coil into a "ball" when disturbed. After acclimating to their surroundings, this trait will cease.

Occasionally found at reasonable prices is the African ball python, *Python regius*. This small species makes an excellent pet, although some keepers feel it is too shy. Photo by J. Dodd.

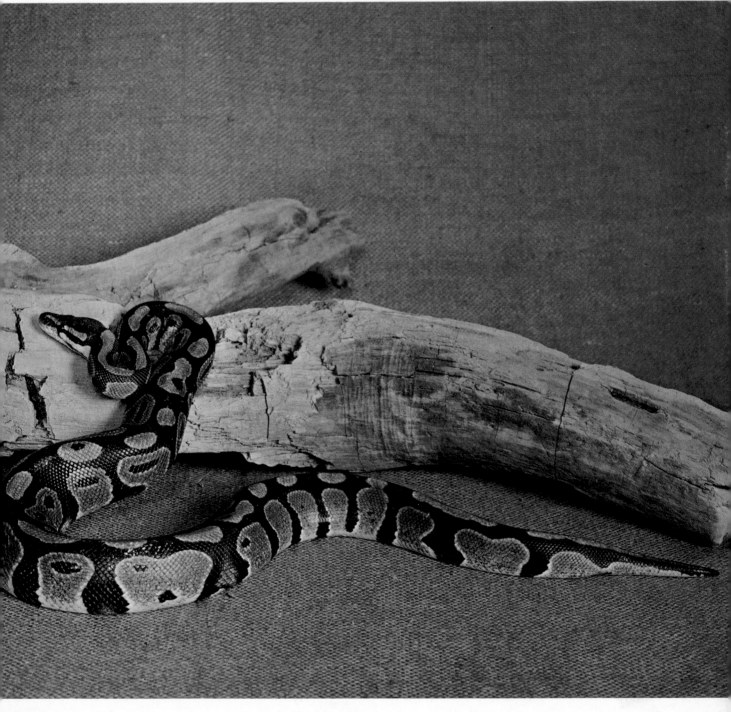

FAMILY COLUBRIDAE

This largest of the snake families comprises about ¾ of all living snakes and about the same percentage of all snakes in the U.S. There are about 350 genera with some 1750 total species. With the exception of the Antarctic, colubrids are found on all continents (very few species in Australia) and range far north through Canada and Scandinavia and southward to the tips of Africa and South America. Most colubrids have a rather slender body form and are quite agile; most can be recognized by having nine large scales on top of their heads. The ventral scales are wide. The family as a whole is considered to be harmless, although several genera are rear-fanged types and at least two African species (the boomslang, *Dispholidus typus*, and the twig or bird snake, *Thelotornis kirtlandii)* are deadly.

Due to the large number of species and the fact that colubrids are the only really common snakes in Europe and the U.S., members of this family are often referred to as "common" or "typical" snakes. However, this family is quite variable, with species that may be either aquatic or burrowers, constrictors or venomous, nocturnal or diurnal, and so on. No matter what their specific adaptation for survival, there are numerous species that make enjoyable pets.

I have taken the liberty to speak collectively when talking about some of the various species of the selected genera. Most mentioned species have relatives that differ in size, color, or range but will still require identical husbandry methods unless otherwise noted. This method will introduce the beginning hobbyist to a wider range of snakes without over-doing the subject.

MANGROVE SNAKE *(Boiga dendrophila)*

This gorgeous tree snake from Southeast Asia can often be found for sale in the more specialized petshops. It is a slender-bodied snake that will grow to be 6 or 7 feet long. It is black or deep dull blue with evenly spaced yellow bands in a "dashed" pattern. Mangrove snakes are rear-fanged, somewhat poisonous, and should only be kept by experienced hobbyists. Mangrove snakes are nervous and may strike at even slight movements. They all require well-lighted cages with plenty of climbing branches and a wide variety of mammals, reptiles, birds, and fishes offered for their diet. They are known to eat other snakes as large as themselves, so it is best to house them strictly alone. An oddity of behavior with these species in captivity is that some are unwilling to ever completely adjust to human touch and will continue to strike throughout their captivity. However, if distracted the snake can be picked up, when it will wrap

Like the other species of mangrove snakes, *Boiga trigonata* is readily assigned to the genus by the presence of enlarged scales along the middle of the back. The head is large and set off from the slender neck, and the pupils of the eyes are vertical. Photo by John T. Kellnhauser.

Although the indigo snakes found in the United States are glossy black animals, in Mexico and tropical America they become more brownish, sometimes with distinct patterns. This *Drymarchon corais melanurus* from northwestern South America shows the black slash mark behind the head that is typical of the subspecies. Photo by John T. Kellnhauser.

around your arm as if it were a branch. If still annoyed it will continue to strike, but not at the arm that it is suspended from, never recognizing it as part of the keeper. Bear in mind that this is a poisonous species; although no one has died from its bites to date, it has made people seriously ill and should be considered dangerous.

INDIGO SNAKE *(Drymarchon corais)*

This is truly an elegant species. It is the longest snake found in the U.S., with some individuals exceeding 8 feet (the record is 8' 7½"). As the name implies, it has a vivid iridescence to its scales to which no photograph can do justice. Indigos are hardy eaters and will accept food items of all types, favoring medium-size rodents. These snakes do not constrict but rather grasp their prey in their strong jaws and press the victim against the substrate. Larger specimens are very powerful but are easily tamed and gentle. Being very active, they should be offered a substantially large cage. Indigo snakes are common in Mexico and Central America, but in the U.S. they are found mostly in southern Texas, Georgia, and Florida. The Florida-Georgia populations are becoming alarmingly rare and are now largely protected (in Florida it is illegal to even possess an indigo snake). Indigos can be successfully mated in captivity, with the females laying approximately a half dozen to a dozen eggs that hatch in about three to four months.

HOGNOSE SNAKES (*Heterodon* species)

The eastern hognose (*H. platyrhinos*) is one of the most familiar snakes in the eastern U.S., but two other very similar species also occur in the U.S. They are readily recognized by the upturned rostral scale (hence the name), stout build, and unusual behavior. They are found most abundantly in sandy and scantily wooded areas. Adults will average 2½ to 3 feet in length.

Hognoses carry out an elaborate stereotyped bluff when disturbed. When encountered in the wild, they first coil the body and flatten the neck into a "cobra-like" pose and hiss loudly and strike with the mouth closed. If the annoyer persists, the snake promptly rolls over onto its back, opens its mouth, fakes convulsions, and plays dead. If righted, it will roll over again, possibly feeling that this should be the correct attitude for a dead hognose. If pestered further, especially if picked up, the snake will void its cloacal glands and regurgitate if it has recently eaten. This behavior is quickly phased out once the snake is settled in captivity. Every individual seems to be tame and harmless, and I have yet to encounter any that bite. Most specimens prefer to hide under a clump of sphagnum moss or in a hiding box

Above: The western hognose snake, *Heterodon nasicus,* is very similar to the common eastern species, differing only in details of head and body scalation and minor but variable color characters. It of course prefers a drier and warmer cage than its eastern cousin. **Below:** *Heterodon platyrhinos* is the familiar hognose of the eastern U.S. Photo above by Ken Lucas at Steinhart Aquarium; photo below courtesy American Museum of Natural History.

Even the more plainly colored kingsnakes usually make good pets. Above is the partially striped color phase of the California kingsnake, *Lampropeltis getulus californiae,* a subspecies that occurs in banded patterns, striped patterns, and intermediates. Below is the Sonoran kingsnake, *L. getulus splendida,* a plainly colored blackish and yellowish subspecies from the southwestern U.S. Photo above by Bertrand E. Baur; photo below by John T. Kellnhauser.

and need only a small to medium-sized cage. The 5-inch hatchlings are common during the spring and fall and can easily be lost underfoot if you are not careful.

Wide variation in color and pattern is found among these snakes, with occasional pinkish specimens, albinos, or solid black specimens being found. However, most specimens will have dark diamonds or blotches in a mixture of brown and yellow. They are good eaters and are highly rated with hobbyists, although to be successful you must have access to a supply of toads or frogs (mainstays in their diets). This can be countered by allowing the snake to hibernate during the winter months and feeding it heavily when its food is seasonally plentiful.

CORN SNAKE (*Elaphe guttata*)

The genus *Elaphe* is a large one that also includes the common rat snakes and black snakes. The corn snake is best known for its long and rather slender form and its bright orange, brown, yellow, and grayish blotched pattern. A strong snake, it is a good climber and should be provided with branches or a lattice. The species ranges from Utah to New Jersey and south to the Florida Keys and can be found in freshly plowed fields and inhabiting abandoned farm houses and barns. There are several subspecies and local forms that vary considerably in color, with the most colorful forms coming from southern Florida. The species of *Elaphe* are inefficient constrictors when compared to the kingsnakes or boas.

Corn snakes and other *Elaphe* species that I have kept survived well on dead rodents that were placed in the cage next to the snake or directly on it as it coiled in its cage. Corn snakes have been known to escape their confines for long periods of time only to turn up unexpectedly and none the worse for wear, needing only to take fresh water. They are active snakes, so give them a large cage. Since they readily accept dead food, it is a good idea to add vitamins in their diet by adding it directly to the body of the mouse. The *Elaphe* species as well as the *Lampropeltis* species are currently undergoing extensive breeding experiments, so new laboratory-produced forms may eventually reach the market.

KINGSNAKES (*Lampropeltis* species)

Aptly suited to their common name, these are truly "kings" among the snakes. They are well-built snakes of medium length (3-6 feet) and are superb constrictors. All will tolerate handling, but from time to time they seem to exhibit nervousness by vibrating their tails rapidly and evacuating the cloacal glands and fecal matter. Fortunately, this display becomes less frequent or disappears after the snakes get used to being touched. This genus contains some of the most beautifully patterned snakes in the world. For example, the milk snakes (*Lampropeltis triangulum*) and mountain kingsnake (*Lampropeltis zonata*) have patterns of red, yellow, and black rings that closely mimic the patterns of the poisonous coral snakes. Others have vivid orange or black and white bands. Still others may be spotted. Though they are rather expensive snakes, many varieties can be obtained through contacts within herp clubs and at better pet-shops. All of the native California varieties (as well as other California reptiles) are now restricted and not allowed to be sold.

Most kingsnakes will eat rodents, but some prefer lizards and snakes. Incidentally, the common kingsnake (*L. getulus*) can easily overcome and devour rattlesnakes.

The milk snakes and similar species of kingsnakes are often called tricolor kings by hobbyists. Above is *Lampropeltis zonata multifasciata*, a mountain kingsnake from California. Below is *L. triangulum syspila*, the red milk snake from the midwestern U.S. Photo above by Bertrand E. Baur; photo below by Ken Lucas, Steinhart Aquarium.

Pituophis melanoleucus is a large (to over 8 feet long) snake found from the northeastern U.S. (New Jersey) west to California, British Columbia, and Mexico. The western races are usually called bull snakes or gopher snakes, while the eastern representatives are called pine snakes. This is a pine snake, probably from the southeastern part of the range. The use of two very different common names for a single species is often confusing to everyone who writes about snakes. Photo by Ken Lucas at Steinhart Aquarium.

Detail of the head of *Opheodrys major,* an Asian species very close to our American green snakes. Photo courtesy R. E. Kuntz.

GREEN SNAKES (*Opheodrys* species)

These very slender, mild-tempered snakes are mainly active during the day. They are good climbers (especially *O. aestivus*) but are often found on the ground. Because of their solid grass green dorsal color they are not easy to spot as they move deftly through the undergrowth looking for spiders, crickets, and beetles. They are often found foraging among tomato plants for worms or coiled on wire fences and looking much like vines. Captives languish quickly if not kept correctly. Keepers must provide these snakes with plenty of green foliage for climbing and cover, plus a wide variety of insects (including but not restricted to mealworms) should be offered. If captured abruptly they may try to bite (their teeth cannot break the skin) but do tame with time. Mating will take place in the spring and summer, and in many instances several females may lay their eggs in a collective burrow. The young will hatch in 6 to 12 weeks and will be more olive drab than green in color.

AMERICAN WATER SNAKES (*Nerodia* species)

The largely aquatic water snakes are found abundantly in the eastern United States. They are excellent swimmers and forage for fishes and frogs in the shallows. If frightened, they retreat to deeper water and display fine subsurface swimming form. The numerous species bear as many as 70 living young that often look quite different from the adults, with brighter colors and more distinct patterns. *Nerodia* species were until recently put in the Old World genus *Natrix*, but they were removed to their own genus several years ago—*Natrix* species lay eggs, *Nerodia* species give live birth. Some of the larger species are commonly confused with the poisonous cottonmouth. Water snakes have vicious tempers and, as scars on my hands will attest, they will bite readily and often. Of course the bites are harmless (though bloody), but captives will remain unpredictable. They prefer live fishes and frogs but may(!) eat pieces of canned fish and fresh fillets in captivity. They are usually good eaters. I have even had a diamondback water snake (*Nerodia rhombifera*) that would accept living and dead mice that had been liberally rubbed with a fish. Other than their usually temporary viciousness, two other drawbacks should be mentioned. Due to their diet, their feces tend to be watery and smelly, so cleaning is a messy and time-consuming chore. Also, although their food is easily obtained, you will have to put up with foul odors from it. Use common sense when deciding where in the house to place their cage. All in all, water snakes are easy to keep, fairly pretty, and eat well. If you persevere they can be tamed and will make good pets.

GARTER SNAKES (*Thamnophis* species)

Garter snakes and their kin, the ribbon snakes, are close relatives of the water snakes and exhibit similar lifestyles and often share common habitats. Perhaps the most common and generally recognized snakes in the U.S., these species average from 18 inches to about 3 feet in length. Although not true in every case, garter snakes are generally noted for being very slender and having yellowish stripes on a greenish background. These fairly aggressive snakes may be found in fields among the high grass or near the edges of ponds. During the spring in areas where garters are very common, cardboard sheets can be placed on the ground (preferably in open fields), on the ground, left overnight, and in the morning nine times out of ten you can find a handful of garters that have sought refuge under these homemade houses. Enterprising youngsters use this method to obtain garters in quantity to sell wholesale to area petshops that obligingly buy them at modest cost. Garters are also being used in numbers for scientific research. Since commercial sellers and users seldom take the time to breed these easily mated snakes, they eventually may drive some species closer to extinction.

When first encountered, garters may flail their tails and whip their bodies wildly. Some will bite, but due to their

Above: Detail of the head of the European water snake or grass snake, *Natrix natrix.* **Below:** Detail of the head of *Thamnophis marcianus,* a garter snake from the southwestern U.S. and Mexico. Notice the similarity in the head patterns of the two species. European *Natrix* species are much more similar in habits to American *Thamnophis* species than they are to the American *Nerodia* water snakes with which they were formerly placed. Photo above courtesy D. Terver, Nancy Aquarium, France; photo below by Ken Lucas at Steinhart Aquarium.

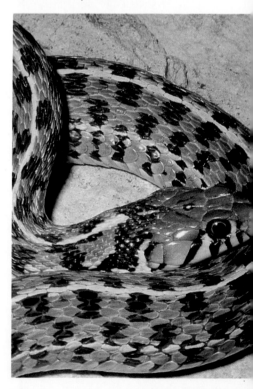

Above: A beautiful albino specimen of the common garter snake, *Thamnophis sirtalis sirtalis.* Albinos are not uncommon in some snake species and are often more attractive than the fully colored snake. Red, yellow, and blue genetic mutations are also found in many snakes and are highly prized.
Below: In North America the racers (*Coluber*) are usually solid colors as adults, with only the young having blotched patterns, but the many Eurasian species of the genus may have brightly blotched or even striped patterns as adults. This is the European *Coluber hippocrepis.* Photo above by Ken Lucas at Steinhart Aquarium; photo below by John T. Kellnhauser.

size this usually will be negligible (though a large garter snake can inflict a quite messy bite). As with the water snakes, they will discharge a pungent-smelling fluid from glands located near the vent and will not hesitate to eject feces. Garters do well in captivity, with the females bearing up to several dozen living young. It is best to offer a wide selection of food including earthworms, frogs, toads, and small fishes. The garter snakes, like the water snakes, seem to tolerate lower average temperatures than many other snakes, usually around the middle 70's.

RACERS *(Coluber constrictor)*

Possibly the most nervous of the common colubrids, racers usually make poor captives where the inexperienced hobbyist is concerned. For ages these snakes have been caught by young boys on hot summer days. Most will bite savagely when first captured and totally refuse food, only to spend the day and night rubbing their snouts up and down the front of the cage. All are streamlined in shape and may vary in color from light to deep blue, black, pearl gray, or pale greenish depending on subspecies. Nervous shaking of the tail can be noticed when the snake is handled. Their body weight must be supported gingerly, as they are fast snakes and always try to move while being handled. They have the habit of biting, leaving their mouth closed with their sharp teeth imbedded in the victim, and tearing the flesh as they pull back the head. A hiding box is a must for all racers and their close relatives, the whipsnakes. I recommend that you leave wild-caught specimens in the collecting bag for approximately 10 to 12 hours and leave the snake completely alone during this period. Then put the open bag into the cage and give the snake the opportunity to crawl out on its own. If kept correctly, racers can live 20 years or more.

I have caught several blue racers of at least 5 feet in length that have had only stumps for tails. More times than not this loss has been due to an unfortunate spell of cold weather. When the snake retreated into its den, it left the tip of its tail partly exposed to the freezing temperatures, suffering frost bite and eventual loss of the dead portion. At least, I think this is a more reasonable explanation than to try to visualize an army of farmers with hoes.

Racer young are hatched patterned with white bands but soon lose this pattern with age. The scientific name falsely implies that they are constrictors; instead, they grasp their prey (birds, mice, lizards, frogs, snakes, and even insects) in their strong jaws and rapidly swallow it. Hobbyists have reported that their long-term captives have readily accepted dead food items also.